The Ribbon Untied
A Journey to Finding a Family

The Ribbon Untied

A Journey to Finding a Family

Ann Eklund

Seattle
2021

The Ribbon Untied
A Journey to Finding a Family

ISBN 978-1-7372117-0-9 Keepsake Softcover

ISBN 978-1-7372117-2-3 Standard Softcover

eISBN 978-1-7372117-1-6

First edition 2021

Printed in the United States of America

The Ribbon Untied, LLC
11905 Venice Loop NE
Bainbridge Island, WA 98110
ann@theribbonuntied.com
theribbonuntied.com

Disclaimer: This story was written from my recollections, research, and memories. To the best of my ability, I have attempted to convey the basic facts as accurately as possible. I recognize that I have interpreted these events from my frame of reference. Of course, there could be other interpretations. This book is not meant to be the only version of the story. Other family members and friends may remember some events differently. Such is the power of memories. We build them based on our unique life experiences and our place in time. I invite any family member or friend who remembers an event differently to write their version of that story and add it to the collection of memories about the Cariker/Taylor/Haines/Blanton clan.

Cover and interior still life photography by Chuck Eklund
Edited by Jennifer Hager
Cover and book interior design by Andrea Leigh Ptak

For My Dear Chuck

To every thing there is a season,
and a time to every purpose under the heaven

—*Ecclesiastes 3:1*

Contents

Introduction

Writing about discovering my husband Chuck's family has been an emotional journey. It is certainly not one I had expected to write. I am not a confident writer of prose, but I desperately wanted to tell Mary Lou's story.

Mary Lou was Chuck's mother. She had him out of wedlock. He knew he was a bastard and was quite proud of it! Chuck was raised by Mary Lou and a stepfather. The only blood relative Chuck thought he had growing up was his mother.

Chuck's stepfather died when Chuck was in his early twenties, and a few years later his mother passed away. He was told very little about any family members. He never knew grandparents, aunts or uncles, cousins or siblings.

But what kept me wanting to know more about Chuck's mother? Why did I start this project? There is a mystery to the whole saga. I wanted to know Mary Lou as a woman who had made it on her own. Why did she make the decisions she made about her son? Basically, I wanted to know what made her tick. What started as my curiosity about Mary Lou gradually evolved into a genealogical quest to find Chuck's family. Could I uncover some of the family secrets? Should I even try to uncover these secrets?

When I started writing about my adventure of seeking Mary Lou's history, I wrote it in the third person, just telling the facts about Mary Lou. The writing fell flat. I was like a distant bystander, recounting the people, dates, and things that had happened, much like in a newspaper article. These facts were interesting, but they did not evoke any emotion or create any sense of Mary Lou's innermost feelings. What was missing was my voice—my desire, my interest, and what I hoped to accomplish. I wanted to portray the discoveries along the journey plus the perseverance and curiosity that kept me focused on the quest.

Working with a writing coach helped me to see that my voice was valued and necessary in order to share all I had learned about Mary Lou. I am the storyteller. In this process of writing, I am reliving much of my own family history. My family had given me a rich, well-defined past of many generations. My family's stories reside in my heart and brain. I wanted to find and give to Chuck his family's stories. Pushing toward this goal, I have spent years researching, uncovering clues, and revealing family histories.

More importantly, in my quest to uncover Mary Lou's history, I have come to understand her essence in my husband. I've learned to see her in the letters and pictures she left behind. And I've found her in our own daughters as they've grown into beautiful, strong women. Mary Lou is part of them all. This revelation came as a surprise. But it has been right here under my nose the whole time.

So, after weeks of trying to tell the story from the outside looking in, I moved inside myself. And from my own perspective, I began to write the adventure of finding Chuck's family. This is that story.

1

Keeper of the Family History

Who is the keeper of a family's history?

When an elder family member dies, how do families decide how to share the treasures that are left behind? There are often legal documents or family trusts that guide the family on how to distribute monies, properties, furniture, jewelry, special dishes, and other valuables. Sometimes there are family disagreements and harsh words. These discussions and hard decisions about dividing up the family resources are usually filled with grief, with a strong overlay of memories about the good times. My family was no different.

I lost my father in 2001, just ten days shy of his turning ninety-three. My father had been the keeper of his family's history. He was the only son with three sisters. Everyone had looked up to him to take care of family business when his family lost their parents. He had enjoyed being in this role. He had excellent organizational skills and planned in great detail. We all joked, but Dad planned his own funeral, down to the music, many months before he passed away, and the service was beautiful! Household finances were in reasonably good shape for my mother to continue to live in their comfortable small townhouse surrounded by all of the things they cherished.

Within a year of my dad's death, my mother fell and broke her hip at the age of ninety. In her gracious spirit, she decided that it was now time for her to move into a senior apartment where she could have better care. She was an active senior citizen and continued her busy lifestyle with church and good friends. The move into her new "digs" with her black cat, "Baby," meant that my sister, brother, and I now had the task of cleaning out the house, putting it on the market, and taking care of the family treasures.

Over several weekends, the three of us, along with our spouses, did the work of removing all of the family belongings and deciding where everything went.

Neither my brother nor my sister wanted any of the antique furniture or the special dishes or silverware. I welcomed it all. I wasn't sure what I would do with all of these precious items, but they would not be sold at the garage sale or go in the trash bin. It was hard for me to understand why my siblings didn't want any of the special family treasures. Maybe, just maybe, I was beginning the role of "keeper of the family history."

Even harder to understand was why my siblings didn't want any of the pictures, keepsakes, and memorabilia. My sister only wanted one thing—my mom's recipe box with all of the handwritten recipes on 4x6 cards. This was really a laugh between my brother and me. My sister did not like to cook, and she and her husband were dedicated vegetarians. Maybe this battered-up metal file box filled with greased-stained cards helped her remember our mom in the kitchen singing and cooking. I, on the other hand, loved cooking, and would have enjoyed having this keepsake. But for family harmony, I was very willing to let it go to my sister.

As we emptied drawers and boxes, we found the pocket watch that had been my grandfather's. As a little girl I had been so intrigued with the long gold chain that was attached to the shiny gold watch that fit perfectly into the little pants pocket next to the belt line. Daddy Pal, as we called him, would take it out and flip open the top. Then he would bend down and show me the time. I can still recall the faint sweet scent of pipe tobacco as he gave me a big grin. The watch had been handed down to my dad and had been promised to my brother. Stored in a satin-lined box, the promised watch was being handed down again. This was the only treasured item that my brother wanted. He and his wife had decorated their house to their own liking and didn't see how any of Mom and Dad's treasures would fit into their house. All the better for me!

As we cleaned out Mom and Dad's cedar chest I, once again, became the family history keeper. Through my grieving the loss of my father, I welcomed all the photo albums, the wedding pictures, the little shoes, the letters to relatives, the family Bibles, the ration books from World War II, the yearbooks, the newspaper clipping describing the beautiful voices of the Kennedy brothers. To me, each item had meaning and held memories of the lives of our relatives. I wanted to know the lore and special stories. I wanted to keep adding to the leaves of our family tree and looking for new roots.

The emptying of the family home did not empty my memory bank of family stories. I had grown up on so many stories. I think as I cleaned out Mom and Dad's house, the flood of memories kept me moving forward.

From way back in my childhood I could remember adventures to visit grandparents.

I knew my paternal grandparents and have vivid memories of visiting their house in Deweyville, Texas. The house stood on brick foundations with a large open crawl space beneath the floors. As kids we would crawl under the house and search for doodlebug holes, twirling our fingers in the holes until we found the bugs. In the back of the house were the chicken coops, always a scary place for me. I didn't like chickens and was afraid they would peck me. My dad would lift me up and put me on top of the smaller coop while everyone else went to collect the eggs.

As night settled, mattresses would be brought into the living room. The floor would be covered to create huge sleeping areas for all the younger grandchildren to have big, rowdy sleepovers. It was a time of laughter and adventure surrounded by loving family members—grandparents, parents, aunts and uncles, and cousins.

I was number twelve of thirteen cousins on my father's side, and I had received the nickname "Pigtail," given to me by Uncle Bonnie. He was a favorite uncle, with a big booming voice and loud laugh. He knew our real names, but he gave special endearing names to all thirteen of us. None of the nicknames were ever used by anyone else. This was an interesting quirk of a fun-loving uncle.

Memories from my mother's side also rushed over me. I have fond recollections of my aunt and two uncles. Both of my mother's parents had passed away long before I was born, so there were no big gatherings. My mother was the youngest of four, and the eldest was Aunt Maisie. My Aunt Maisie took on the role of the matriarch, always inviting us for family gatherings at her home. The usual choice for dinner was ham with all the homemade fixings. The baked sweet potatoes with toasted marshmallows were always my favorite.

Over the meal we would hear family stories. The most intriguing one was about my grandfather, the town's postmaster. In 1916, my grandfather was murdered as he walked home for lunch! My mom was only four when her father was killed. The stories continued with tales about how my grandmother took charge. As angry and sad as she must have been, she moved with the four children to a small farm in East Texas, which my grandfather had recently purchased. My mom always said they were very poor—but never hungry.

One of my favorite stories was about my mother churning butter. As a young girl she would sit on the front porch of the farmhouse and move the butter whip up and down. The faster the whip moved, the sooner the butter would form. My mother loved to sing and would sing as she churned. She would always laugh with a twinkle in her eye as she told us, "And every now and then, Mother would tell me, 'Mary, sing a faster song.'"

I had grown up on these stories that were told over and over at Thanksgiving and Christmas dinners. For me, these stories mean family and caring and loving. I never grew tired of hearing them.

All the friends I had growing up seemed to know their roots and had connections with family. We all had our own family stories that wove the generations together and gave context and stability to the family. It is hard to imagine not knowing anything about your ancestors, or at least your grandparents and their history.

I had never known anyone who didn't know about the roots of their family, until I met Chuck.

2

The Love of My Life

*I*n the summer of 1962, when I was fifteen, my parents and I moved from the flatlands of a big city in southeast Texas. As a high school student in Texas, I traveled a few miles to school through rush-hour traffic with my best friend, Susie, in her Corvair. Growing up, I had a wonderful childhood and early teen years with many friends and an active social life. I enjoyed school and participated in student government, serving as a class officer. My outside life was filled with piano lessons and singing in choirs. As a young teenager I was an active participant in youth activities at a very large Southern Baptist church. When my family left Texas, my friends gave me several going away parties. Susie said she had a hard time believing where I was going. How could my family leave all of this behind?

My parents left behind the pressures and politics of a big-city school district and an overpowering Baptist church. My dad left behind his aging mother, three sisters and their husbands, and all those cousins. My mom left her sister and brother and their families. It was difficult for all of us to leave our family and friends, but my father's physical and mental health depended on making a new start.

We moved to a small rural community in Central California. The beautiful rolling hills covered with oak trees and dotted with cattle seemed to be medicine for our souls. My brother and sister were off to college back in Texas, so I was the fortunate sibling to move with my parents. Once we arrived in our new home, my parents began teaching in a three-room school in a small ranching community. Dad was the principal and taught math to all grades, 3–8. Mom taught the reading and literature to grades 3–8. They team-taught all the other subjects. Their excitement about their new jobs seemed to energize them. The students and parents loved and appreciated them and even teased them about their Texas drawl. They were creating an environment of learning that helped children succeed.

I was in a different world as I started my junior year of high school in California. I now rode a school bus for over an hour through the winding mountain roads to get there. I had to get up early to be ready and get to the village post office to meet the bus at 7:00 a.m. Off to school and home again by 5:00 p.m. My new world included making new friends and attending dances, which I had never been allowed to do in Texas. I learned to ride horses and help with cattle roundups. My parents and I attended the only church in our community. It was a different denomination in a very small white-steepled chapel set against the oak trees.

As my parents and I looked back on that move, we would say, "It was the best thing that could have happened to us." They were healing, and we all became CITs—California Improved Texans.

As I reflect on my move as a teenager, I wonder how I made the transition. It all seemed unreal—being plucked up from the rich life I lived in Texas and plopped down into a totally new environment. All I can say is that the mountains and the rolling hills spoke to my soul. I loved the seasons with the occasional snow, the people, the newness, the adventure of it all. I don't remember being sad or lonely or missing my Texas friends. I was living a new life, and one which I found thrilling.

My parents and I quickly made friends and felt at home. Mom and Dad were amazing educators who loved their work. In the spring of that first year in our new home, they were asked to work at the children's camp for the summer. The camp was just seven miles from our home, high up in the mountains on the edge of the Sequoia National Forest. They would accept the position only if I came along to work with them.

My first summer in California, the summer of 1963, was one of magic for me. Here I was, a young sixteen-year-old, working at a summer camp in the mountains in California. Coming from the flatlands on the Gulf of Mexico, I never would have dreamed of this life.

It was in this place that I met Chuck—the future love of my life!

I was sixteen and Chuck was nineteen. Chuck had been coming to this summer camp since he was eleven years old and had been a counselor for several years. The camp is a working ranch owned by a family. The young campers and the counselors all slept out on metal cots under the heavens filled with stars. The days were packed with activity. Summer in the mountains of Central California is glorious—warm summer sun, almost no rain, and crisp, cool evenings.

My job was to help supervise children ages six to thirteen. We rode horses, swam, hiked, went on overnight campouts, sang camp songs, and harvested fresh vegetables to have for dinner. I was exhausted every night as my head hit the pillow, and my muscles often ached from so much activity. But as a young girl meeting new challenges, I was never happier.

Meeting Chuck made the summer even more perfect! I had seen him at a distance at the small community church a few months before camp started. He was with Ross, the son of the owners of the camp. This new guy was tall and handsome, dressed in cord jeans and a button-down blue shirt, driving up in a cute little sports car. Ross and I were friends at school. So, the next day at school, I asked Ross, "Who was that with you at church yesterday?"

Ross quickly smiled and said, "Oh, that's Chuck. He came up for a weekend visit. He works as a counselor at camp during the summer." I can remember thinking that the summer job would not be so bad after all.

My first recollection of meeting him was that he made a comment—one that I have never let him forget. We laugh about it to this day. I was often teased about my strong southern accent. When another counselor called me "a real Southern belle," Chuck replied, "yeah, a real ding-dong!" But in a few weeks, I guess my southern charm captured his attention, and we had our first date before the camp was over in August.

Camp ended, and Chuck returned to Southern California. I went home to start my senior year in high school—riding the school bus and seeing my friends. My first letter came on August 29, 1963. (*Here it is, just as it was written.*)

Dear Ann

I miss you very much.

Its Wednesday, it boring, its hot, humid, *smoggy, noisy and slow. Everyone moves at half the speed I have been accustomed to for the last ten weeks. They move only a quarter as fast as you though. All in all, its a pretty uninspired day. The only decent place around is the beach, and thats great. Only bad thing is I haven't been there yet. My friends say its been great thought, so I guess they are right. I have been extremely busy, sleeping, which is great way to rest, which is what

*pronounced with a cough and tear

II

you will probably feel like doing by the time you return from your arduous journey.

Speaking of journey I imagine you are in or leaving Oklahoma City, and on your way to Texas, to visit all of your old boy-friends (pangs of jealousy). If I have any luck they will have all defected to Alaska, not being able to stand living in the second largest state. In fact theres a rumor going round that the only people left in Texas, are a few old people, to weak to make the trip to Alaska. And about 30% of the ?sidewinders? or side-winders

III

who are poorly educated and can't read. I can hear your answer already. "Never!"

Just now I was remembering our last night together. I was surprised by your honesty. Most girls when told they were loved, would answer back that they loved too. Either out of habit, embarrassment, or because they think its the proper thing to do. I can't help it, as little security as your answer gives me, it makes me love you all the more. and when and if you do tell me, you love me, I'll know it to be the truth. Thinking about you makes me happy and sad at

IV

same time. Sad because I'm not near you, happy because I love you. its supposed to be bad to tell a girl your hooked, but the hell with technique, it makes me sick sometimes.

So good-bye little one, I will see you soon.

Love, Chuck

P.S. Thank you for the card. I'm starting a mountain with the dirt.

I am not sure how I reacted when I received this letter. I "liked him" so much, but my upbringing had taught me to be a proper young lady. And what did I say in this situation? I think I just ignored the emotion and pretended like it never happened.

Chuck knew my parents because they'd worked at the camp for eight of the ten weeks also. And over my senior year in high school, he would drive his cute, bug-eyed Sprite up to the mountains for visits. He would spend weekends at our house. So he would hear family stories firsthand from my mom and dad. He would hear in detail about our life in Texas. My parents thought he was terrific and always welcomed him for visits.

Over the course of many months of dating, Chuck began to share about his family. I had never known a family who shared so little history of their relatives. He knew nothing about grandparents, nothing of aunts and uncles and cousins. He did know that he had been born in South Bend, Indiana, and that his mother had brought him to Southern California when he was a toddler. He knew his mother had been an army nurse at Pearl Harbor when the Japanese bombed it. But she never shared about family and had no contact with them.

One of his most painful memories was about how he had been physically abused by his stepfather. As Chuck shared the story, he was very matter-of-fact about the events, showing little emotion. Chuck's mother and stepfather both worked at the veterans hospital. She was a nurse and his stepfather a security guard. They had the same shifts and went to and from work together. When they arrived home, the drinking would begin and continue through dinner until his stepfather would fall asleep. Several hours later, his stepfather would wake up in a rage. He would beat Chuck's mother first and then head down the hall to attack Chuck. This behavior might happen several times a week with seemingly no pattern to why or when.

On one particular night when Chuck was around seven, he and his mother were able to get away from the hits and yelling and hide in the bathroom. As Chuck sat on the edge of the bathtub and his mother sat on the toilet seat of the very tiny room, they listened to the raging outside the door. This was the night when she chose to tell him about his real father.

"That son-of-a-bitch is not your real father—your real father was a pilot, and shot down in World War II in the Pacific."

This was all his mother ever shared about his father. I was only the second person Chuck had told about the abuse. He was nineteen when he shared it with me. What must Chuck have thought after the tirade was over, as he and his mother crept out of the bathroom and scurried to bed?

As I reflect now, I wonder what a young Chuck would be thinking as he lay there in his bed. How did it change his behavior and feelings toward his stepfather and his mother?

It was difficult for me to comprehend this type of abuse. I was very naive and sheltered and had never heard about this type of behavior. But I knew I didn't want to share this with my parents. I knew enough about the world, and abuse was a deep secret. You might not want to associate with someone from that kind of family. I think I was afraid they would say I couldn't date him. So, I kept the secret, too.

I see Chuck's sharing of this event as a pivotal moment of trust in our relationship. I think he shared because he wanted me to know and because he knew he could trust me with the secret.

Our romance continued through most of my senior year of high school. We saw each other every few weeks. Either I rode the Greyhound bus and stayed with married cousins close to where Chuck lived, or he came to the mountains and spent the weekend at our house. We shared so many adventures! When I would travel to see Chuck, we would go out on dates all over the Los Angeles area in his cute little Sprite with the top down. We drove to Malibu and Zuma beaches, visited folk music clubs, enjoyed movies, and ate hamburgers at the Hamburger Hamlet or yummy sandwiches at My Brother's Bar-B-Q. We traveled all up and down Ventura Boulevard. I met his best friends, Mike and Jeff, and often double-dated. Chuck would sometimes surprise me with special concerts at the Greek Theatre or the Hollywood Bowl. He opened my eyes to the beauty of Southern California—from its beaches to the mountains. We tootled around in his convertible car with seemingly few worries. This was a very far cry from the young girl who had left Texas less than a year ago!

In all these adventures, Chuck took me to his house only once, and I met his mother and stepfather for just a very brief time. The impression was fleeting, but I do recall that his stepfather was a good-looking gray-haired man with a soft voice and friendly smile. As he said hello, I could detect a strong Swedish accent from his homeland. Chuck had shared that his stepfather, as a teenager, had immigrated from Sweden. His mother gave me a quiet hello and a quick smile. They didn't ask me any questions or seek to engage me in conversation. Maybe I was just there to let them see who was dating their son. This was the extent of my contact with them.

During my many visits together with Chuck, he had shared his desire to join the army. Maybe that desire came from knowing that his father and mother had both served in the army in World War II. It wasn't a surprise when I received a letter telling me that he had enlisted.

He left for basic training in the late spring of 1964. I was busy with activities as a senior in high school. Our communication continued through his training with lots of letters and great detail about his impressions of the army. After basic training and advanced infantry training, he was deployed to Berlin. The letters were less frequent. Chuck spent eighteen months in Germany, and he volunteered to go to Vietnam. The letters became more frequent again, and very angry at what he was seeing. At one point he said he wanted to "wash this dirty war off."

While Chuck was serving in the army, I went off to college. My eyes were opened to new ideas and new people. Over the next two and a half years, the connections and threads of love were always there through our letters. However, we both stretched our wings and kept our independence. We dated and fell in and out of love with a few others along the way. We were never ones for "going steady."

I was still spending my college summers as a camp counselor at the same camp where Chuck and I had met. Late in August of 1966, I received a letter from Chuck. He had returned from Vietnam because his stepfather had died in his sleep from a heart attack. Chuck would have leave for a month before returning to duty.

He contacted me after the funeral. We saw each other often during these few short weeks he was home. His mother did not drive, and during the course of this month, he helped her take driving lessons and buy a car. Slowly she adjusted to her new life alone and continued working as a nurse.

Chuck returned to Vietnam and I returned to school for my junior year of college. I hated the fact that he had requested to be deployed to Vietnam! I was becoming more active in the antiwar movement, and I didn't understand. He had explained that he wanted to see what was going on for himself. But I was worried. Chuck had shared the dangers of war and the statistics of how many soldiers had been killed a few months before their discharge date. So now my antiwar protest activities seemed to have even more relevance. I knew and loved a soldier who was in that horrible war.

I am not sure what changed in my heart, but after this visit, I realized how deeply I loved him.

It was hard to tell him how I felt because I was afraid he had fallen out of love with me. Just maybe he could tell that my feelings had grown, because our letters became more frequent. We began to express hope of spending future time together. His army discharge was coming the following spring. I think he had even started a "short-timers" calendar, counting off the days until he was discharged. We continued to write—and write and write!

Chuck was discharged from the army in the spring of 1967. He was flying into Travis Air Force Base. From the base he would go into Oakland, California, and complete all the necessary paperwork for his exit. From Oakland he would come by train to Davis, where I was in the spring quarter of my junior year at UC Davis.

I was so excited to see him again! I had bought a special dress—a pink and green floral A-line linen dress. I dressed with care as I anticipated seeing him. With the long, loud whistle announcing its arrival, the train from Oakland to Davis rolled in. I can remember feeling the butterflies in my stomach. I wasn't sure how I would react. When I spotted him, I started running toward him. It felt a bit dramatic and romantic, but oh, so good to be wrapped in his arms!

After a short overnight visit where we stayed with friends in an off-campus apartment, he flew home to Southern California. The letters continued; he started back to school the following fall semester to begin college with a serious focus. Meanwhile, I transferred from UC Davis to UC Berkeley for my senior year, and Chuck would drive to Berkeley every few weeks.

As I reflect on this time in our lives, I realize this is when I began to know Chuck's mother. She stayed quietly in the background with little to no drama. Occasionally, I would come to visit and stay at Chuck's house. Usually, we would go out to dinner with his mother. When I arrived, Chuck would have my room ready. I do not recall his mother ever doing anything to welcome me—but she'd say hello. Unlike my mother, who would have been at the door with a big hello and smells of special goodies coming from the kitchen, Chuck's mother would usually be in her room listening to the radio, surrounded by her dogs. Flicka, the boxer, was usually at the foot of the bed snuggled up with Bight, a cute black-and-white mixed breed that Chuck had introduced into the house. Lying next to Mary Lou was her favorite—Luta—also a mixed breed. Mary Lou had selected this special puppy from a little girl who was giving away puppies outside the grocery store.

Over the course of many months, Chuck's and my relationship and love grew stronger. Both of us became comfortable now sharing our love openly, and we began to start talking about getting married. There was no big down-on-your-knee proposal—it just evolved and happened. But if we wanted to get married, I needed to get a job after I graduated. Chuck was committed to getting his degree, and fortunately he had the GI Bill to help financially.

During this time, teachers were in very high demand, and I could start to look for a teaching job without having a California credential. With a bit of luck and some great coaching from my teacher parents, I was successful in finding a job.

In the fall of 1968, I started my first teaching job in Bakersfield, California, about 100 miles from Chuck. This was just about perfect. The letters stopped and the phone calls began. We were able to see each other every weekend.

During my weekend visits to Chuck's house, we would go out to dinner with his mother—always to the same place and for the same meal. The pattern of going to dinner with Mary Lou was my only real contact with her. She had one special restaurant—The Golden Bull—in Studio City. The restaurant was one of the many iconic steak houses of the 1950s scattered along the miles of boulevard in the San Fernando Valley. It was decorated with red upholstered booths and dimly lit with some candles on the tables. The smell of years of people smoking permeated the air.

Almost every meal was the same—a cocktail of scotch for her, a Tom Collins for both Chuck and me. The meal would start with a relish dish of carrots, celery, and a few olives, along with a basket of warm bread. Mary Lou then would light up a cigarette as we proceeded to order. We would all order a green salad—with Thousand Island for Mary Lou and ranch dressing for us. Mary Lou would have a rare steak with baked potato and lots of butter. Steak was usually our choice, too, but well done. And we liked our baked potatoes with sour cream and chives added to the butter. We ended with coffee, and Chuck often sipped French cognac in a big brandy snifter while Mary Lou smoked another cigarette. Over dinner, the chatting would usually be about the weather or something that had happened in the world of politics. She also loved the Dodgers baseball team and had the latest information on the season and players.

Our waitresses were the same each week. It was like visiting with friends as they greeted us and made us feel welcomed.

Mary Lou was always very kind but distant.

After my first year of teaching, I was fortunate to be offered a teaching job close to Chuck. This was so exciting because it meant that we were able to plan our wedding.

Over the summer of 1969, I moved into our future apartment in the San Fernando Valley. I handwrote wedding invitations to our family and a few dear friends. During the weeks of planning, Mary Lou asked me to go to Bullock's Department Store with her to buy her dress for the wedding. I was surprised and honored. I remember having a great time with her as we looked at dresses and laughed and shopped. Her taste was very classic and tempered—no wild colors or details. She settled on a beige and white, color-blocked dress with a small belt etched with gold. She bought brown shoes and a purse to round out her ensemble. At the wedding, she and my mother, who dressed in pale green, were perfectly coordinated in early fall colors.

Simplicity was key, as Chuck and I did almost all the planning together on a very slim budget. We were married on a very hot Labor Day Monday, September 1, 1969. My father walked me down the aisle. As Chuck and I met, we each gave red roses to our mothers. Chuck's former college English teacher read poetry from Kahlil Gibran's *The Prophet.* Dear friends Ross and Ed sang favorite folk songs and played their guitars. Our minister friend was performing his first wedding, and he read the beautiful chapter from the Bible on love—I Corinthians 13. As we said our vows, we were surrounded with love by my parents, Chuck's mother, my sister and sister-in-law, and a few close friends.

After a toast of champagne and cake cutting, we were ready to be on our way. We headed off in my parents' camper with Chuck's motorcycle strapped to the front for a weeklong honeymoon. Finally, we were together.

Chuck Eklund, US Army, 1964.

L to R: Ann Cariker Eklund, Chuck Eklund, Mary Lou Eklund (mother of the groom).
Ann and Chuck's wedding, 1969.

L to R: Marion Cariker (father of the bride), Ann Eklund, Chuck Eklund, Mary Cariker (mother of the bride).
Ann and Chuck's wedding, 1969.

The Ribbon Untied

3

Getting to Know Mary Lou

*C*huck and I settled into married life. I started my second year of teaching in a new school district. Chuck had completed his first two years of community college. For his junior year of college, he transferred to the state university in the San Fernando Valley, California State University at Northridge (CSUN).

Our life was full of work and school and many moments of laughter and fun times with friends. We had very little money, but it didn't matter; none of our friends had too much more.

Like many of our friends, we had furnished our one-bedroom apartment with big pillows, a card table and chairs from Blue Chip Stamps, and bookcases made of cement blocks and boards. Usually, the biggest investment was the bed, and a few of us had televisions. We had great parties carving pumpkins and eating chili, or wine and cheese parties where each person had to bring something he or she had created—a song or poem, a piece of pottery, a loaf of bread. We all sat around on the floor piled with pillows and talked about the world.

In our minds in the early 1970s, the world was filled with chaos and discord. The news was filled with the horrors of war and distrust of our political system. Many of us had marched and protested against the US involvement in the Vietnam War. Chuck had witnessed the war firsthand, and he, too, marched. He felt the war would be over soon. Among our friends we wondered about the wisdom of bringing children into the world we were living in. We all shared the desire to work to make it better.

On reflection, life was simple, even with all the problems. We were idealistic young people building our love and our lives together.

Against this backdrop of our married lives, I had regular experiences with Chuck's mother.

As I recall these experiences, I realize that my memories are meshed into a few years. I had my own personal experiences with Mary Lou, but most of my information came from Chuck telling me things he remembered from his youth. At the moment that any information about Mary Lou's earlier life came to me, I didn't see the relevance or big picture. Only on the looking back do I see and maybe understand how our daily lives affect how we perceive the world.

We would see Chuck's mother almost every week for dinner. There was usually no other contact. This pattern of weekly dinners had started when Chuck and I were dating. We continued going to the Golden Bull and would occasionally venture out to the Hamburger Hamlet or a Mexican restaurant. Over our meals, we would chat about our lives, me as a teacher and Chuck's adventures in college as a geography major.

Never once did we talk about Chuck's childhood or Mary Lou's life as a nurse. It was a missed opportunity, and one I wish I could replay. Who was the keeper of the family history in Mary Lou's family?

Chuck did know some basic facts. He doesn't have too many memories of when he was told certain things, but over the years of his growing up, Chuck's mother had told him she was born in South Bend, Indiana, and had an older sister. Her mother had died when she was younger, but her father was still living. In Chuck's recollection, there were never any visits, phone calls, or letters coming from either his aunt or his grandfather.

Another distant memory was about train tracks. Chuck doesn't recall what prompted the telling—maybe they were waiting for a passenger train to pass and he showed interest in the train. But he thought he remembered being a young child and crossing over tracks. He asked his mother about this.

Interestingly, she told him that they had been on the wrong side of the train tracks in a train station in Chicago. This would have been after they'd left their home in South Bend and were traveling by train across the country to California. Mary Lou and little Chuck had to hurry off the platform and run across the rows of train tracks to the other side. It was late in 1946, and Chuck wouldn't have been even three years old!

As I think about this story, I can imagine a young woman tightly gripping the hand of her toddler son, racing to get to the other track. It seems like Chuck's bringing up this memory would be an opportunity for Mary Lou to talk about Chuck's life as a little boy in Indiana. But Mary Lou was not one to add any detail to the story. Maybe it was too painful for her.

This cross-country train trip from South Bend was taking his mother to work as a nurse in the Wadsworth Veterans Hospital in Santa Monica, California. World War II would have just ended. Nurses were in demand, and hospitals were busy places. There were few apartments or houses available, so the hospital provided nurses' living facilities on the grounds of the hospital. Chuck laughs as he recounts this. He thinks he was probably spoiled by all the other nurses and had lots of care and attention.

Chuck has little memory of getting to know the man he called "father." He was only four years old when his mother started dating Gustav Edvard Eklund. Mary Lou had met him at the veterans hospital where he worked as a security guard. Chuck had seen pictures of himself with his mother and Gustav at the beach, but he has very few memories. What Chuck knew about his stepfather's early life were just the facts that had been shared over the course of many years. Gustav Edvard was born in Sweden, left home as a teenager, and worked his way through Europe. Eventually, he immigrated to the US and joined the Seabees. Later, Chuck would discover that Gustav had been married and had a son. Apparently, Gustav was in the service when he received a "Dear John" letter from his wife wanting a divorce.

Chuck assumed that Gustav was his father because Chuck's name was Charles Edward, and his stepfather's name was Gustav Edvard. So Chuck thought he had been named after his father. It wasn't until he was seven and hiding in the bathroom to get away from his stepfather's abuse that the real story came out.

Mary Lou and Gustav were married in 1948 in Nevada, and Chuck was legally adopted in November 1950. His name was officially changed to Charles Edward Eklund.

I'm guessing that in those days, having a different name than your father's family name was not socially acceptable. This also gave Mary Lou a reason not to have to explain about who Chuck's real father was.

By 1951, Mary Lou and Gustav had settled into their married life and purchased a small house in the San Fernando Valley in the greater Los Angeles area. So many soldiers were returning from the war, and housing was difficult to find. Developers were busy ripping out orange groves to make room for new houses. The postwar economy was booming, and families were growing. Chuck's family was able to purchase a small house in the city of Encino. The house sat on a corner lot surrounded by other houses, close to schools, and a few blocks from the busy main thoroughfare of Ventura Boulevard. It was a neighborhood filled with lots of families and plenty of places to roam.

This was the house in which Chuck lived for over twenty years as he grew from childhood to manhood. But if the walls of that tiny house could talk, the stories would be painful with not too much joy.

The stories that Chuck's mother told about her life were few and far between. As Chuck and I dated and later married, he would share the tidbits that he remembered.

The one story that Mary Lou told in great detail was about her service as a nurse at Pearl Harbor. Mary Lou had been on duty on her birthday (December 6, 1941) and was in the operating room (OR) that night. So the celebration would be the next morning over coffee. Many of the nurses were gathered on the veranda of the hospital overlooking Pearl Harbor that morning— December 7, 1941. Mary Lou would recount that they first heard the sound of fighter planes. However, this wasn't unusual because the Army Air Corps pilots liked to flirt by "buzzing" the nurses who sat out on the veranda. Maybe over the birthday song the women could hear the roar of engines. "Happy birthday to you, Happy birthday to you, Happy birthday, Mary Lou, Happy birthday to you." But this time, they could see the Japanese planes! One pilot came so close, he pushed back the cover of the plane and looked over at the nurses. This was for real.

Mary Lou also shared that as a result of the attack, she had shrapnel in her leg. And she showed the scar to Chuck. But again, no mention of his father even as she shared these events.

Through the years, other interesting facts of her life would emerge. Chuck doesn't have a recollection of how this sharing would take place—probably just the two of them being together. Maybe something like a news item or the cover of a magazine would spark the conversation.

Another fascinating story she told was about her experience of going to see the premiere of *Gone with the Wind* in Atlanta. This adventure occurred while she was in army nursing training. In great detail she told of the glamour of the evening and where she was sitting. She could even *see Margaret Mitchell*—the author of the book!

Mary Lou also talked about dating some of the Mafia persons who lived in Chicago. Chuck remembers seeing a *Life* magazine that showed faces of some of the mobsters. *Life* magazine was part of Chuck's memory, and he and his mother always enjoyed reading the features. On one particular day, the magazine arrived with a feature story about the Chicago Mob. Mary Lou looked at all the mug shots of the mobsters on the front of the magazine. In a somewhat blasé manner, she told Chuck that she had dated this one and that one. "And," she said, "they weren't 'bad' people." We have no evidence that she actually dated any of these men. But she did attend Cook County Nursing School in Chicago, so who knows?

She also shared that she had worked as a nurse at the Studebaker factory in South Bend. It seems that she worked there briefly after Chuck was born in 1944. Chuck loves this connection to old car models. And of course, he knows the history of Studebaker, founded in 1852, and maker of wagons, buggies, carriages, and harnesses. I loved hearing this story as Chuck told it to me, because my brother and I learned to drive our stick-shift Studebaker when we lived in Texas.

For Chuck, probably one of the strongest connections with his mother was their love of reading. Mary Lou was a voracious reader. She belonged to the Book of the Month Club. When Chuck was in the fourth or fifth grade, she would let him choose books he was interested in and order them for him. Chuck was struggling with learning to read, according to his teachers, and this seemed to pique his interest. The first book he got was a story of the history of the marines. It was very difficult reading. So he used the dictionary to help him with the words. The next was *John James Audubon* and much easier. So, after he had mastered this book, he returned to the story about the marines.

Mary Lou did not enjoy cooking, and Chuck's stepfather almost always made dinner. Gustav's Swedish meatballs were one of Chuck's favorites. Chuck cooked the Sunday breakfast of eggs and pancakes. Mary Lou was basically a meat-and-potatoes person—no fish, no chicken, no rice.

Mary Lou had some very interesting jewelry. One pin that Chuck recalls was a small vial that held water and a fresh flower. Gustav had landscaped their new home with beautiful climbing roses that covered the chain-link fence that surrounded the house. Gustav would cut her a rose to place in the small vase. Since she wore a nurse's uniform every day, this would be something special.

Chuck does have memories of his stepfather taking him on weekend excursions—Jungle Land, Catalina Island by plane, and the new Disneyland. However, Chuck's mother never went with them. There were a few camping trips when all of them went to Yosemite to stay in the tent cabins.

When Chuck reminisced about these events, there was always a level of anxiety about his stepfather. He would share the excitement of the activity but never any thoughts of "Gosh, I loved doing all those things with my dad!"

Even though Chuck had these few bits of family history, they were just facts. Maybe when Mary Lou shared with her son she could put herself back into the scene of the moment, but emotions didn't seem to carry into the story. There seemed to be little joy or happiness.

It has been interesting to me to think about what made Chuck grow into a well-rounded, highly intelligent, caring man with an amazing sense of humor. The family dynamics were strained and stressful. But Chuck somehow managed to forge his own path and develop his own sense of value and worth.

Chuck would tell you that there were several special people who supported him along the way. When Chuck was in sixth grade, he was held back for a semester—"flunked," he says. In his new class he met Mike and became best friends. Mike's mother, Barb, unknowingly became a cheerleader and supporter of Chuck's. Chuck spent many hours at their house, swimming and playing Monopoly and other challenging board games. Barb seemed to see the potential in him. She would tell Chuck that he was "so smart!" He had never heard that. In fact, his stepfather often called him stupid. Barb cosigned a loan for Chuck to buy a guitar when his parents wouldn't help.

I knew I needed to pass muster when I met Barb for the first time. I wore the same pink and green linen dress that I had purchased for Chuck's homecoming. When Barb greeted me, she said, "Oh, Chuck, she is so beautiful!" I guess I passed. In the months after that initial meeting, I came to see the Barb who cared for Chuck. She was a hero to him, and she didn't even know it.

The other persons who affected Chuck most were the Jamesons, owners of the summer camp where Chuck and I met. Rod and Catherine were the most unique people. They were straight with you; they offered encouragement. They listened to you and valued you as an individual. Chuck had gone to camp every summer from the time he was eleven. So, for the next seven summers, he was under the influence of these caring adults.

Because I had worked at camp with Rod and Catherine, I could see firsthand the influence they had. Camp was a safe place to just be yourself, work hard, and make mistakes without fear of violence. Your efforts were rewarded with kindness and appreciation of a job well done.

Neither Barb nor the Jamesons knew how powerfully they had impacted Chuck. As he and I began to date and share our dreams together, he was able to look back and see that these adults had modeled behaviors that he had emulated. His core being was given a chance to thrive under their care.

As I watched and interacted from the eyes of a young girl in love with Mary Lou's son, I came away with my own set of recollections, particularly of Mary Lou.

Mary Lou didn't seem to have any friends with whom she connected. She loved her dogs, and they seemed to be her companions. The dogs were with her always. The dogs were all buddies and played together. Usually, Luta was curled up on the bed with Mary Lou as she smoked and listened to the radio or read. The yard was fenced so the dogs had lots of room to roam and just be dogs.

Unlike my mother, Mary Lou visited the beauty parlor every week and had her hair and nails done. She wore her hair in a short curly style. Her pictures in her youth showed much the same style. Her nails were always beautifully manicured with dark red polish, and she continued to wear her wedding band even after her husband Gustav had died. On her right hand she wore a beautiful big jade ring, an oval cut surrounded in gold. One day when I was alone with her, we were sitting in the living room on the small sofas and just visiting. I'm not sure how the conversation came to be, but I shared how much I admired the jade ring. She told me she would like me to have it. I assumed that meant when she died. Again, no history of where or how she had acquired the ring. Never knowing that her death would come sooner than we ever imagined, I so wish I had asked more about the ring. And about so many other things.

Since I have always loved clothes, it was interesting to me that Mary Lou didn't keep very many clothes. Maybe it was because she had worn a nursing uniform for work for so many years. When she did purchase something new, it was beautiful. She would order from or shop at Bullock's, a top-end store that carried classic clothes and lovely home goods. One outfit I remember well was a lovely dark blue skirt with a color-coordinated silk blouse that had a subtle design. She had worn this outfit almost every time we went out to dinner. Mary Lou had a Coke-bottle figure—with a small waist and shapely bust and hips. As I look back at her pictures from the nursing days, her figure seems to have stayed the same for years.

My most unusual memory was of Mary Lou's smoking habit. She was a chain-smoker for sure. But the routine was like nothing I had ever seen. In her purse, or by her bed or chair, she had *three different kinds* of cigarettes—one non-filtered, one menthol, and one filtered— Pall Mall, Salem, and Tareyton. As she smoked, she would rotate the order and smoke one after the other. She never seemed to forget the order. She had shared with Chuck that she started smoking around thirteen. When we went to dinner, the cigarettes were always in her purse. Since smoking was allowed in restaurants, she would continue her routine and smoke with our cocktail, between courses, and certainly with coffee at the end of dinner.

When holidays rolled around, my parents would always include Mary Lou in our family dinners. I recall one Thanksgiving when Chuck and I took her with us to my folks' home. They had by now moved from the mountains to the Mojave Desert. Mary Lou didn't like turkey, so she offered to bring a ham. My mom was so gracious as she heated the canned ham and added all the fixings. I am guessing that Mary Lou had not had too many fun-filled holiday dinners like we were used to having. She was always quiet and polite. She was gracious as a guest and appeared to enjoy being included.

As I look back on Mary Lou's life, I think that in today's terms, we might say she was depressed. I never remember any discussions about feelings or the sharing of emotions. She simply just existed in the moment.

Even though I might have worried about her accepting me as a daughter-in-law, I think she thought that Chuck had "done all right." I never remembered hearing her tell us that she loved us, but we always ended the evening with a peck on her cheek and sharing our love for her.

Mary Lou was certainly a person of routines—seemingly never to venture too far from her usual norm. But as I look at her life and what we have discovered, this is not the same Mary Lou I imagine in her twenties.

In the last week of November 1971, Chuck and I arrived at our usual Sunday evening "going out to dinner" time. As we pulled into the driveway and up to the chain-link fence, Chuck realized that the *Los Angeles Times* Sunday paper had been left outside the gate. He stopped abruptly and jumped out of the car; he bounded over the fence and ran into his old home. There his mother lay in her bed—she was able to tell us that she had fainted the day before. Once she regained consciousness, she had crawled to the phone to call for emergency help. The firemen came, found her, put her back in bed, and tried to call us. In those days, there were no answering machines on the phones, so no message was left! Chuck and I had been out on Saturday evening, so she lay in her bed with the three dogs around her for almost twenty-four hours. As she described to us how she had passed out, it was obvious that she had had some type of seizure. She was lucid but very weak. There was never any question about the need to get her to the hospital.

The next moments were frantic. She was able to walk, so we carefully placed her in the car and quickly fed the dogs. We rushed her to the emergency room of the neighborhood hospital, where she was admitted. Chuck and I were in stunned silence. Everything happened so fast! And now what? Over the next several days, Mary Lou stayed in the hospital and underwent many tests. A brain tumor was detected. She had no health insurance, so staying in the neighborhood private hospital was not an option. But her doctor knew that she was a veteran with health benefits. Could we get her to a veterans hospital? The doctor—bless him—was able to get her admitted to the Wadsworth Veterans Hospital in Santa Monica. With no funds for an ambulance, Chuck and I transported her and helped get her settled in a new bed. The hospital had very few rooms for women, and she was placed in a ward with several beds. Interestingly, this hospital facility is where Mary Lou had worked as a nurse for many years, and here she was again.

As I look back, I wonder if this was a comforting place for her. She had seen many hospitals and knew the routine. Things that seemed strange and a bit terrifying or overwhelming to Chuck and me were possibly normal to her.

Within a few days, the new doctor performed surgery intending to remove the tumor. The doctor was gentle and kind as he gave us the news. The spot where the tumor was located was inoperable. We were in a state of shock as he told us that she had "from one month to a year to live."

Over the next few days, Mary Lou was recovering from the brain surgery. She talked and visited with us, and for a while she seemed to be bouncing back to normal. I don't think Mary Lou was told directly, but I sensed that she knew she was seriously ill. Chuck and I, still in our twenties, had no experience talking with anyone about death and dying.

We visited every day after work. It was a long drive through rush-hour traffic over the Sepulveda Pass and then back home. Chuck was doing his student teaching and was very busy with planning. To help make ends meet, Chuck also worked as the maintenance manager at our big apartment complex. I continued teaching.

During the first week Mary Lou was in the hospital, we moved from Newbury Park in Ventura County back to Mary Lou's home so we could take care of the dogs. We didn't know how long she would live, but we wanted to bring her home even for a brief time. In the spare moments we had, we decided to paint and clean up Chuck's old room and have the twin bed—with new sheets, pillow, blanket—all ready for her.

A few days before Christmas, we decided we wanted to decorate her area of the ward. There were very few other patients, and Mary Lou had a bed at the end, next to an old window that was no longer in use but now barred and closed off. The nurses were kind and reassured us that we could bring things in to make the area more festive. Chuck and I selected a small living Christmas tree and decorated it with small, beautiful bulbs and shiny strands of gold beads. Our plan was to plant the tree in her yard after Christmas. We were hopeful that this would bring her some cheer. For a few brief moments she smiled and laughed with us about the tree. She still wanted her cigarette, and we would light it for her. Then after the first puff, it would sit in the ashtray on her bedside table. Conversations were hard. We were seeing her slowly decline and unable to remember too much.

In early January 1972, we had everything planned for her to come home for a few days to see the dogs. We brought her home late in the afternoon and set her up in her new bed. The dogs were so excited to see her and crowded around her on the bed. We thought we could take care of her—including her eating and hygiene needs. We didn't even last through the night! Around 2:00 a.m., she asked if she could go back to the hospital. With heavy hearts we packed her up in the car. For the last time, we drove her back over the road she had traveled many times, back to the hospital where she had worked for more than twenty-five years. We felt like we had failed, but maybe the hospital was more of a home to her . . . maybe she was more comfortable there. She never came home again.

She drifted into a coma around January 14, and again we visited every day. The nurses had moved her into a private room by this time. On the morning of January 20, Chuck received a call that the end was near. He went to the hospital and sat by her side all day. I went off to work with my mind thinking about him and his mother. He left the hospital knowing that she would probably not make it through the evening, but he chose not to be there. He came home, and we went to a school board meeting in the district where I worked. The elementary teachers were asked to attend this meeting to show support for children's freedom to choose appropriate books. A parent was trying to get *Charlie and the Chocolate Factory* removed from the library. The whole evening seemed surreal, but we just didn't want to be at home. When we came home, Chuck called the hospital and heard the news. His mother had died. We lay down in the middle of the floor with the dogs around us or sat in different parts of the living room, just antsy as we talked through the night and mourned the loss of his mother. In the middle of the night there was a knock at the door. The veterans hospital staff had sent a telegram confirming Mary Lou's death.

Our orderly, organized life had just taken a new turn. What would the future hold? Chuck had no family. I was his family. Mary Lou was gone, and there were so many questions to ask her. Would we ever know her feelings, her secrets, her life as a nurse, her childhood in Indiana?

Was there anyone who cared except Chuck and me?

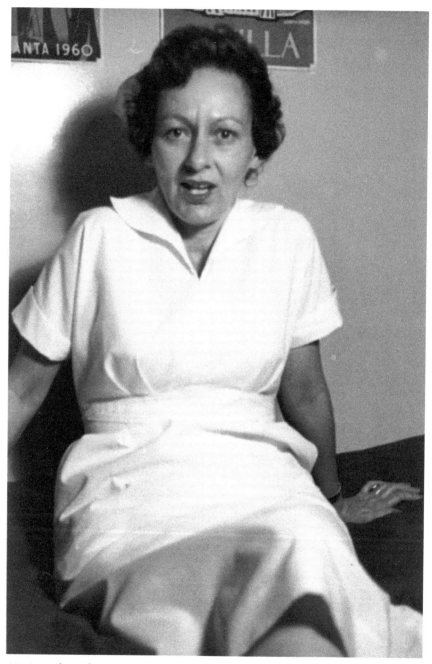

Mary Louise (Haines) Eklund. Nurse at Wadsworth Veterans Hospital, Santa Monica, California, c. 1960.

The Ribbon Untied

4

The Secrets in the Closet

On January 20, 1972, Mary Lou died peacefully in her sleep in the Wadsworth Veterans Hospital in Santa Monica, California. At the age of fifty-nine, she had died from lung cancer that had metastasized to her brain.

Mary Lou was awarded a military service ceremony with a fourteen-gun salute at Rosecrans Military Cemetery in San Diego, California. My parents and some dear friends, Frank and Jackie, traveled to San Diego to be with us. For the interment, the six of us stood around the casket on the hillside that overlooked the Pacific Ocean. The American flag was draped across the coffin. Very carefully the soldiers removed the flag, folded it in the proper protocol, and handed it to Chuck. He had stood with his mother at this same spot five years previously when his stepfather was buried at this same grave site. This time, it was a sad moment for a life cut too short. Even though Chuck and I had my family and our friends around us, we felt very alone.

In a few days, we were back in our work and school routines. The reality of being adults who had to make decisions without the help of older family members around hit me hard. In my mind, I was still the baby in the family, and my parents were the ones who made these tough life decisions. Diseases that killed and growing old were not part of my life experience. Chuck had not made these types of decisions either. However, his resilience and his desire to move out of his family home were strong forces.

We began the difficult and painful process of cleaning out Mary Lou's small, post-World War II house. Chuck had lived in this house as a child and teenager. It was not easy. The memories were still raw. We stored our few possessions in the garage and tried to make ourselves feel comfortable.

The house was clean but dingy. It smelled of *years* of cigarette smoke and being a home to three dogs. Green carpet from the '70s covered the living/dining combination room, and sectional furniture bordered the walls. In one corner was a beautiful antique oak rocking chair with a few dog-teeth marks on the runners. There were three tiny bedrooms with hardwood floors and a very small bathroom. The kitchen was just big enough to have a small vinyl-topped table and three chairs. The big corner lot was surrounded by a cyclone fence covered with climbing roses, and there were lots of large trees and bushes across the back.

Each weekend we resumed the cleaning process to get the house ready to sell. There was no consideration at all of keeping the house and living there; the unhappy memories were too strong.

As we cleaned, we found old jewelry, several Swedish bibles, a set of *The Works of Shakespeare*, odds and ends of kitchen tools, an old rolling pin, and a hand juicer. In one drawer we discovered a $12,000 government-issued life insurance policy. It appeared to be just another piece of daily mail along with old checkbooks and other financial information that had never been organized.

But the real treasure was in the closet of Mary Lou's bedroom.

The closet was designed to be like a cabinet with a bottom shelf set several inches off the floor. Along with the dust bunnies, I pulled out Mary Lou's old white nursing shoes, the brown pumps she had worn at our wedding, and several old boxes. But tucked back in the dark corner was an old shoebox covered with years of dust. I peeked inside, not knowing what to expect. There were letters, documents, and pictures. I think the moment I opened the box I could feel something special. I excitingly called to Chuck, "I think you may want to see what's in this box!"

We took the box into our bedroom and sat down on the edge of the bed. Chuck slowly began to lift items from the box. A picture of a man in uniform. Some baby pictures. Some legal papers . . . and a stack of letters tied with a red ribbon.

Chuck gently untied the red ribbon.

All the letters were addressed to 2nd Lt. Mary Lou Haines, ANC. We could quickly see that the letters were organized by date in their original envelopes.

These letters and documents opened up a whole new world about Mary Lou. The world of Mary Lou that I had known for the past several years seemed to vanish in the face of the contents of this dusty old shoebox. It seemed that the secrets inside were just quietly waiting to be revealed.

On opening the letters, we realized they were from Chuck's real father, whom he had never met. (Here they appear *just as they were written*, mistakes and all.)

Mary Lou Darling,

Maybe you will receive this sooner than you did the last one—I'm getting up at 03000 to give it to the pilot of a PBY that is returning to Oahu. I think the reason you received the others late is because they were held over here, or maybe on Oahu. We don't have a ship out of here for there every day you know. I could write a letter and have it lay over here for 3 or 4 days.

Well Butch, it's definite this time. I will be back on Oahu some time between the 12 and 18 of this month, I've seen the order. I will also have a least 5 days leave coming up soon as I report in. We probably be stationed a Kanoehe, or maybe Shafter.

Here is my idea of how I would like to spend my leave. If you could arrange to have your leave start at the same time that mine does we could do the Island of Hawaii together. If you can't do that get any time after the 18th and I will try to get mine to start then too. (at the same time) I will cable you as soon as I know the day of return for sure. The number that I mention in the cable will be the date of arrival, no matter what the cable says. Code, get it. As soon as you get the work you can start making arrangements for your leave. Try hard, darling—I am in desperate need of a vacation and it will be much happier if I can spend it most of it with you.

Until I can see you,

Love,

Chas

4 Jan 42

This was the first letter, written in January 1942, just a month after Mary Lou had been celebrating her birthday on the morning of the bombing of Pearl Harbor. Chuck and I sat on the bed and excitedly opened letter after letter. The information just kept coming. Was this man really his father? Who was the man in the picture? The documents showed Chuck's original birth certificate from a hospital in South Bend, Indiana, and his name was Charles Edward Taylor, Jr. There were also adoption papers to indicate that Chuck had been adopted by Gustav Edvard Eklund who had married Mary Lou in 1948. Chuck had never seen any of this!

What was the story he had been given? He had never been told about his real father or shown any pictures. His memories were of Gustav's abuse and of that night he and his mother had hidden in the bathroom.

As we opened the letters, painful emotions of the abuse came back to Chuck. He could put himself back in the bathroom with his mother, sitting on the edge of the bathtub and being told that the man outside the door was not his real father. And now, in the same house, just a few steps from that very same bathroom, here is Chuck, some twenty years later, opening letters that may be from his real father.

Against this backdrop of not knowing who Chuck's father was, we carefully pulled each letter from the envelope, one letter after another. And an image of his real father slowly began to come into focus. The picture of the man in uniform *had* to be Chuck's father. We couldn't stop reading—not too much sleep that night—as we talked and wondered. The shoebox filled with treasures showed us a new Mary Lou and the man she loved, just waiting to be found.

Mary Louise Haines. Location unknown, c. 1935-36.

The Ribbon Untied

5

Mysteries in the Shoebox

$\mathcal{T}$he shoebox is where all the mysteries began. The secrets started to peep out. I can put myself back in the place of sitting on the floor or on the edge of the bed reading the letters for the first time. Excitement, wonder, questions, and being aware of Chuck's reactions of stunned amazement. So many unanswered questions! But now—so many pieces of the puzzle about Mary Lou and her life!

In Charlie's letters to Mary Lou there is no clear statement that he accepted that Mary Lou's son was his. In his letter of July 8, 1944 (a few weeks after the baby was born), Charlie writes this:

> *You have never given me the details of your leaving the ANC. I know that you have wanted too far some time. For goodness sake break down that tremendous reserve that you use to seal yourself off with and tell me about it.*

And in the next paragraph:

I hope to be back in the States by Xmas at least. I certainly intend to see you then if you are in South Bend or Chicago. Be sure and let me know where you will be and before I forget it note the APO 244 Hq. 1318th Fighter Group.

Let's not forget to write each other, Butch. I think of your constantly and certainly want to know what is happening to you.

Love,

Chas

In the letters between July and October of 1944, Charlie mentions "little Slug" several times and even comments on pictures she has sent.

The pictures of the kid looks fine. I think he looks a lot like his mother. Of course the pictures don't show his face very well. He doesn't look as if he had any hair to spare, does he?

September 23, 1944

And in the final letter dated October 1944, he writes:

I think I'll be back in time to mush up to see you about Xmas, OK? I want to see you very badly. I have a lot to talk over with you.

What does your sister and Dad think of young slug? Does he pass inspection? (Not the Army kind yet, I hope.)

And the last line of the letter:

Good bye darling until I see you.

Love,

Chas

I have read and reread the nineteen letters from Charlie and cried and cried. His love of Mary Lou was evident, and he still wondered about her. What happened to the love between Mary Lou and Charlie? Why wouldn't she share more honestly about the baby? Why did she bring her son halfway across the US and *never tell anyone* where she was going? Why did she bring the shoebox filled with the secrets? Why didn't she tell her son even after he was older? The questions go on.

I only have one side of the story—one set of letters from Charlie. But not Mary Lou's responses.

However, another perspective came into view from other letters that were in the box. These were from 1st Lt. James O. Ballou—it seems he knew both Charlie and Mary Lou. In this letter dated May 13, 1945, he says:

> I got your letter post-marked 25 April today. It said what I was afraid it would say. However, I will say this about Slug, Sr., he is a pretty intelligent gent even if he is a very spoiled little boy. If Slug gets the training his old man so obviously needed and missed he might be quite a boy at that.

Then the second letter from Ballou—almost a year later, April 16, 1946:

> It has been one hell of a long time since I have heard from you, I recognize that as my entire responsibility, however. I didn't use very much tact, nor amount of understanding I have in writing my last letter. I should have known better than to take the attitude I did about Slug. I'm sorry and I shan't do it again.

There were five more letters from May until the final letter, August 12, 1946. In these letters, James tries to convince Mary Lou to come to him in Longview, Washington. He will be a father to her son and help her get a job at the local hospital. He shares in great detail about the beauty and weather of the Pacific Northwest. In the last letter he says:

> *I am quite disappointed that you are not coming out to this country to live.*

And once again he tries to convince her to come to Seattle or Portland. But later, in almost the last paragraph of this two-page letter, is one of the most telling statements that seems to confirm the true identity of Mary Lou's son.

> *No wonder you didn't want to tell me Slug's name. You really have had a hell of a time trying to get Charlie out of your head, haven't you? Still, I do feel a bit as though you gave him a rough deal. Women are so awfully hard to understand. They won't stand hitched to any one idea unless you want them to change their minds and then they are obstinate as mules. I suppose that that is a part of their fatal fascination though.*

It is through these letters that we discovered a Mary Lou we did not know. This gift from the shoebox would change our lives. I can imagine her holding tight to her son's hand as she rushed that young toddler over the train tracks while balancing luggage. Bigger items, like the shoebox, probably came in a trunk.

The letters, pictures, and legal documents had been carefully packed. Why didn't she destroy the evidence of her child out of wedlock? She deliberately carried those letters across the country and placed them in a special spot in the closet. She hadn't managed to tell Chuck more than that single sentence when he was seven years old. But she left the letters carefully organized and tied in red ribbon for him to find. She couldn't express her love openly, but she left her son this amazing gift of love—his history, his roots, and the joy of love between two people—Mary Lou and Charlie. Just maybe, *she herself*, was the keeper of the history of this small family.

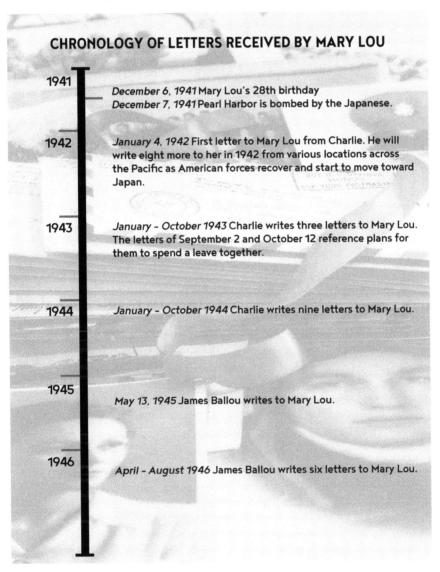

CHRONOLOGY OF LETTERS RECEIVED BY MARY LOU

1941

December 6, 1941 Mary Lou's 28th birthday
December 7, 1941 Pearl Harbor is bombed by the Japanese.

1942

January 4, 1942 First letter to Mary Lou from Charlie. He will write eight more to her in 1942 from various locations across the Pacific as American forces recover and start to move toward Japan.

1943

January – October 1943 Charlie writes three letters to Mary Lou. The letters of September 2 and October 12 reference plans for them to spend a leave together.

1944

January – October 1944 Charlie writes nine letters to Mary Lou.

1945

May 13, 1945 James Ballou writes to Mary Lou.

1946

April – August 1946 James Ballou writes six letters to Mary Lou.

Charles Edward Taylor.
Photo from c. 1940-41 was found in shoebox with letters in 1972.

Capt. Charles E. Taylor with crew and P-39 Airacobra, somewhere in the Pacific Islands, c. 1942.

6

Building Our Family

The death of Mary Lou and the discovery of the letters from Chuck's real father were major pivotal points in our lives. The small life insurance policy had been issued to Mary Lou, and Chuck was the benefactor. After redeeming the policy, we could use some of the money to begin to clean up the house to put it on the market.

Throughout the spring of 1972, Chuck was completing his student teaching and I continued my teaching. Weekends were busy with cleaning and sorting everything in the house. Chuck wanted to keep very little, but we did decide to keep the antique rocking chair with dog-teeth marks on the runners and an antique desk with chair.

I carefully looked through all the dishes, silverware, pots and pans, and cooking utensils. The silverware was interesting with some initials on the silver-plated forks and knives, but none that tied to the family names. There were a few collector's spoons, and I wondered if these were from Mary Lou or Gustav's travels. I chose to keep the silverware and a few vintage utensils like the rolling pin and hand-cranked orange juicer.

Thinking back on these few things, I have wondered where they were acquired. Mary Lou had carried the letters across country. Did she also bring any home goods? Gustav was the one who did the cooking, so the utensils must have been his purchases. The furniture pieces were some of Chuck's favorites. He especially liked the rocking chair, but again, he had no memory of when or how it was brought into the house. The rocker and the antique desk have traveled with us in all our moves. Maybe these beautiful pieces make me think there were times of calm and caring in Chuck's home.

To this day I take out the rolling pin and use it. Forming a piecrust or rolling out biscuits always makes me think of this early time in our marriage. I find myself wondering what kind of pastry Gustav might have made. I also found a few linen napkins and a matching tablecloth. These I have added to my linen stash, and they get used for summer dinners on the deck. It seems like keeping a bit of this past history is important to me.

Chuck and I decided that a yard sale would help us get rid of the many unwanted items. One weekend early in the spring of 1972, we were up at the crack of dawn dragging out all of the items to be sold at the yard sale. A neighbor whom Chuck had never met appeared and started asking us questions about what was going on. We shared about Mary Lou's death and told him we were getting the house ready to sell.

Well, the house did not even get put on the market! Before we had finished the yard sale, the neighbor reappeared with his sister and told us she'd be interested in buying the house. What a special surprise!

We didn't even have to talk with a realtor. The attorney who was helping us with the probate was able to help us with the sale of the house. Within the week, we had the property in escrow. This seemed to be just about the perfect solution—selling to a neighbor's widowed sister who also wanted the dogs!

We had planted the Christmas spruce tree from Mary Lou's last Christmas right in the middle of the front yard as a memory to her. This dear woman who bought the house was so kind. She assured us she would leave the tree.

Unfortunately, when we were working on the house, one of the dogs escaped and was hit by a car. It was Luta, Mary Lou's favorite. It was so hard to see Luta suffer. She couldn't be saved, so we had to put her to sleep. It seemed that Luta needed to be with Mary Lou, wherever she was. Flicka and Bight would be able to grow old in their own home with a new owner who would probably love them as much as Mary Lou did.

All the pieces fell into place as we were ready to walk away from this chapter of our life and Chuck's past history.

While we were busy preparing to move out, we were also looking for a place to purchase. With the small insurance money and the profits from the sale of the house, we now had enough for a down payment. In our spare time on the weekends, we found a new condo that was under construction. It seemed perfect. New, clean, and a dramatic three-storied floor plan.

Chuck had been offered his first teaching job. With our meager savings and both of us now receiving incomes, we were barely able to qualify for a loan. But unlike many of our friends who were still in apartments, we were taking a really big step.

Construction of the condo was completed, and we took ownership in September 1972. A new chapter was beginning. We still didn't have much furniture, but the card table and the cinder-block bookcases were things of the past! It was an exciting time to be shopping for furniture and starting to build for our future.

During the two years we were living in the condo, the housing market started to boom and prices skyrocketed all over Southern California. Chuck was alert to this trend, and he suggested that we might want to move closer to our jobs—and into a larger house. With the equity we had acquired in our condo, we moved again.

By now we had welcomed two cats into the family mix. We were fortunate once again in finding a one-story house with four bedrooms and a large yard. It was a typical suburban house within the boundaries of the school district where Chuck had a job. My teaching job was just a few miles down the road.

We were the typical young married couple, just living our lives with all the other young couples. Our weekends were spent laying a very large brick patio, with built-in planters for roses, and landscaping the yard. The population of school-age children was on the rise, and there was a huge demand for teachers. Chuck and I were fortunate to have many friends in the teaching profession, and we all helped each other—moving into new houses, building fences, laying sod in our lawns. Almost none of our friends had children.

Our decision to start planning for a family was filled with emotions. We certainly didn't come into marriage with any expectations of having children. In fact, we were so worried about the conditions of the world that bringing children into such a chaotic environment did not seem like a responsible thing to do. Most of our friends felt the same. However, our parents' generation seemed concerned by these points of view. Often, they tried to tell us that the world had always been fraught with problems. Children would bring many blessings. We listened and pondered.

My memories of growing up in a caring family were positive and happy. Chuck's memories were often of the abuse. Would he carry on the cycle of abuse? He certainly didn't think so, but we talked and talked about this question.

We decided that the first step was to get a dog and practice our parenting skills. Oreo was a beautiful, big, copper-colored malamute—related to the Siberian husky breed. She put us through our paces with her boundless energy. She ate up all the rose bushes and destroyed her big doghouse! When we came home from work, we never knew what we might find. But slowly, her loving nature matured and captured our hearts. She mellowed into a gentle giant. Through all of this, Chuck kept his calm and began to realize that an abusive nature was not part of who he was.

During these years we would often talk about Chuck's mother and the finding of the letters. Would we ever know what happened?

In the summer of 1975 on a lazy hot afternoon, one of Chuck's teaching colleagues, Buffy, was over for a visit to see our new "suburban" home. She and her husband were close in age to us, and they were buying their first home, too. We had all become good friends. As the conversation rambled, we told her about the letters from Chuck's father. We also mentioned the Ballou letters and wondered out loud if we could find him. We expressed that James Ballou could be a clue to finding out what happened to Chuck's father.

That put Buffy into high gear. Her father had been a manager with the phone company, and she knew the ins and outs of getting information.

We quickly moved from the garden atrium on the brick patio to our family room. But to get close to the phone, we had to sit on the floor. Phones—even the modern push-button ones—were connected by short lines to a wall outlet. Our "modern" phone sat in the corner of the family room on a stereo speaker. We still had very little furniture, so we pulled the phone around the corner into the dining area, and all of us plopped down on the 1970s gold shag carpet and spread the Ballou letters out in front of us.

First, Buffy took charge. She called the #411 information operator in Longview, Washington—no James Ballou. In the letters to Mary Lou, James Ballou had mentioned that he had a brother in the Sacramento, California, area, so why not try the brother? Again, Buffy called the #411 information operator, this time in Sacramento—and there he was. She found the number of a Dr. Ballou, a psychiatrist.

It was now Chuck's turn. Buffy and I sat listening as Chuck called the office of Dr. Ballou. The receptionist answered, and Chuck tried to put into a few sentences the nature of the call: we had found these letters, and we were looking for the doctor's brother—James Ballou—who knew Chuck's mother and father. Buffy and I were making eye contact and holding in a laugh. It all sounded so ridiculous. We imagined that the receptionist was probably rolling her eyes and wondering if this *kook* on the other end of the line was for real! But being a gracious receptionist, she said she would give the request to the doctor.

As Chuck hung up, we all broke into laughter at the whole saga and thought we would never hear from the doctor.

But to our astonishment, he called. Chuck again laid out the story about finding the letters and wondered about finding his brother. Dr. Ballou shared that his brother had died, and that he had no knowledge of Mary Lou and Charlie. But he did offer to ask his sister, as he was heading to Indiana to visit her family in the next few days.

Our hopes of getting somewhere in our search were both heightened—and then dashed—as we never heard from him again. So, this one small sliver of connection was gone.

Our only conclusion at this point was that Charlie had died in World War II. Just as his mother had indicated on that painful night, locked in the bathroom.

Chuck would often tell his friends this story of finding the letters. Then he'd share the adventures of his mother at Pearl Harbor. He enjoyed being teased about being a bastard. None of our other friends could match his family history.

This episode with the Ballou letters piqued our interest in finding out more about Chuck's father, but we didn't dwell on how or when we could find any further information. We were very involved with our careers and starting to think about having a family. Our emotions about the world were starting to temper as we believed that we could be good parents. Without telling our friends or family, we decided that we wanted to bring our own children into the world.

By the late summer of 1975, I was pregnant with our first child. And we were ecstatic. It seemed that many of our friends were going through the same transformation, and there were babies on the way! Our child would certainly have lots of playmates. Baby showers were common. Shopping for baby stuff and decorating the nursery were high-energy activities.

Our family histories came into our minds as we started thinking about names. My sister and I both had middle names that were the maiden names of our grandparents. My sister, five years older than I am, was named Mary Page. My maternal grand-mother was Buelah Page (Kennedy). And I was Ann Rush—my paternal grandmother was Willie Seaman Rush (Cariker). These leaves on the family tree had grounding for me.

There were no sonograms to tell you whether your baby was a girl or boy and no gender-reveal parties. Along with our friends, we just wanted healthy babies. Naming children is always fun. We had our share of laughs as we combed through the books of names—Prunella was out! Bringing in Chuck's history was a given. The box of letters had revealed Chuck's real last name—Taylor. We agreed immediately that we wanted to use Taylor as either a boy's first name or the middle name for a girl. Using this name felt like we were carrying a part of the family history into our generation.

Maybe someday we would find out more about the Taylor side of the family, and our child would come to know that history. As we prepared for our firstborn, the names we chose were Jennifer Lee (my father's middle name) or Taylor Lee. Our Jen arrived and was given her name.

Then nineteen months later we were choosing names again—and again, no sonograms or hints from the doctor about gender! We chose another girl's first name and still Taylor for a boy's first name. But since we had already honored my side of the family with Jen's middle name, we could put another girl's name with Taylor. Our daughter arrived, and she was given the name Rebecca Taylor. She loves the name and the story that goes with it.

Our small family was complete, and the family names with a little bit of history would continue.

Chuck and I both had been raised in families in which our mothers worked outside the home. My mother was a teacher and

Chuck's mother a nurse. I truly enjoyed my job and wanted to have it all—motherhood *and* my career. Both of us had seen this modeled. Chuck was extremely supportive. We worked hard to build in time for our young daughters in the midst of our teaching careers. We shared the family workload and took turns with dishes and bedtime routines. Fortunately, we were able to find quality childcare, which made our teaching careers even better. So many of our friends now had children, which filled the weekends with birthday parties and christenings! It was a busy time.

Our family memories included much time spent with my family. My parents had retired from their teaching professions and moved within a few miles of us when our Jen was born. As my mother would say, "The realtor didn't sell us the house, your Jen did." They were perfect grandparents—not too nosey or demanding. They were there for us as we built our new family. Through the years, our house or theirs would be the meeting place for family gatherings. My brother and his family would join us for special events and holidays. Jen and Rebecca were delighted to mix with their cousins. My sister and her husband would also come for visits.

Within a few years of starting our family, Chuck's antennae went up again on the housing market. Our girls were still young when we found another great new house—two stories with a big bonus room above the garage. The neighborhood was growing with lots of kids, and a new elementary school was being planned within a few blocks. Our current house sold very quickly. But our new house was not ready for us yet. It was January of 1979, and we had to move out of the old house.

My parents came to our rescue.

The happenings at my parents' small condo have been the topic of many fun-filled conversations. Mom and Dad had purchased a two-bedroom condo with a small eat-in kitchen and small living/dining room. A small patio connected the house to the carport. It was perfect for them and their dog. How do you put four more people, one large dog, and two cats into the mix?! My dad was always the planner and problem solver. If we could move from a thirteen-room house in Texas to a four-room house in California, then this was doable!

Mom and Dad gave Chuck and me their master bedroom. We put our king-sized mattress on the floor. The room had a big walk-in closet with just enough space for Rebecca's crib. Mom and Dad took their bed to the guest room and stayed there. Jen slept on a small cot on the floor at the foot of their bed. The dog and the cats were put in a kennel. Our furniture was packed into storage, and houseplants completely filled the small patio. We made it work!

Every weekend Chuck and I would take the girls to visit our dog and cats. The girls both had the chicken pox during these months, and Mom and Dad were there to help with childcare. Jen fondly remembers snuggling up with her grandparents, and she would say, "Tween you, Grammie and Grandpa." Rebecca loves the stories of her sleeping in the closet and sliding down the stairs on her belly as she laughed with delight. When Chuck and I would talk with my folks and share our appreciation for their support, they would say, "That's what families do." It was a special time.

Fortunately for all of us, Mom and Dad had already booked a monthlong trip to Italy before our move-in date, which would give us their house for a few weeks by ourselves.

Over the next four months we all laughed and cooked and played together. These everyday life events bonded us even closer to my parents.

Once we were in our new house, it was again time to land-scape and build the block wall fences. All the neighbors and many friends would pitch in and help each other. Our lives seemed very full. What else could be added to the already full plate?

Within the first ten years of our teaching careers, Chuck and I were both asked to take on leadership roles. Was going back to school even a possibility? We would both need to have master's degrees if we wanted to move into administration. We began talking to my parents about getting our master's degrees and administrative credentials. How could this work?

I remember my mom saying, "*This* is the time to go back to school. If you wait until the girls are older, they will be so active that you won't have the time. *Now*, you can put them to bed and go off to night school or study." She was so right.

They helped us financially so we could go to a private univer-sity that was closer to us. This would limit our travel time for night school. Chuck and I tried to schedule our classes on alternate nights so that one of us was always home with Jen and Rebecca. Mom and Dad were our support team on this new journey to continue our educations.

Chuck started the degree program in counseling with an additional credential in administration. He had been told that if he had his master's degree within a year, he would have a job. He was able to fit in all the coursework, and that job as a middle school counselor was his. I took a step back and slowed down my coursework. So within two years, I had my master's degree and administrative credential.

Completing this phase of our formal education laid the groundwork for our futures in education. Chuck went on to become a high school principal and district office director of

The Ribbon Untied

secondary education before retiring in 2006. I, too, became a principal, district office coordinator of curriculum, and then the director of elementary education in one of the districts in which I worked. I retired from public education in 2007.

Through all these steps and job changes we raised our two daughters. Chuck and I both were asked by our bosses to consider continuing our education to earn a doctorate degree. Every time, we said *no*. We truly enjoyed our jobs at the school sites, and we were not willing to devote more time to study and less time with our girls. No. Our family time was precious and valued.

The girls were typical kids with homework, music lessons, dance lessons, Girl Scouts, and lots of activities with friends. When I became a principal, it was obvious that we needed some help with the home front. We looked at different options and finally decided to hire a Swedish au pair. For the girls it was like having a big sister. Each year for three years, we would have a new au pair arrive—Ingala, Mona, and Susan. Then we hired Amparo, an immigrant from Mexico. We taught her English, and she taught us some Spanish. Once the girls were out of elementary school, we hired a teenager who would come to our house every afternoon to be there with the girls until either Chuck or I arrived home.

These were very busy times. On reflection, though, I think Mom and Dad were so proud of Chuck and me. They didn't gush and tell us. But they were there and simply offered their love and support to our lives and the decisions we were making with our family. By the way, years before, they had learned of Chuck's background of abuse. My fears of telling them had certainly just been in my head. They never questioned Chuck's love for me or his moral integrity—not for a minute.

Some of our most valued family time was when we traveled. During the summers we would have adventures all around California, exploring the Gold Country, Disneyland, Yosemite, and San Francisco. Other special experiences were trips to the Pacific Northwest, riding ferry boats and walking the Butchart Gardens in Victoria. Over the winter breaks from school, we planned short special trips. The San Diego Zoo coupled with the Norman Rockwell Exhibit was another memorable adventure.

But one of our most favorite memories was going to San Francisco after Christmas to shop the "after-holiday" sales. We would usually stay in a downtown hotel so we could walk everywhere. On this particular trip, we had all gotten into our pj's to watch TV after a day of sightseeing and shopping. Then Chuck started thinking that he'd like some hot chocolate. "Well," I said, "let's go to Ghirardelli Square and get some!"

Within minutes we were all up. We just put coats on over the girls pj's and rushed out to jump on the cable car. The cold wind off the San Francisco Bay was exhilarating. Riding the cable car at night was magical with all the holiday lights! Hot chocolate (without whipped cream) for all of us. It was a night to remember.

When the girls were still young enough to believe in the Easter Bunny, we took a trip over spring break with my parents to a big family reunion of my dad's side of the family in East Texas. Chuck and the girls had never *seen* so many aunts and uncles and cousins! We visited my girlhood stomping grounds, sharing all of the fun family stories and history. Mom and Dad were thrilled to be able to share their kids and grandkids with the Texas families. The girls remember that the Easter Bunny found them—even in Texas!—as chocolate eggs were hidden all over their grandparents' hotel room. I think my accent came back within a few minutes of the plane touching down in Houston. And before we left Texas, I'm sure that Chuck and the girls were saying "Y'all."

When the girls were twelve and ten, we took them to Washington, D.C., and the surrounding areas. Chuck knows so much history! He could keep the stories alive and interesting. We ate dinner in Christiana Campbell's Tavern in Williamsburg, where George Washington had eaten. But the real showstoppers were the *lightning bugs*. Jen and Rebecca had never seen them before and made delightful screeches of excitement every time they saw a bug light up.

Our girls were great travelers. They were troupers who complained very little. The family rule was that they could bring along one doll or stuffed animal, and they had to carry one small piece of luggage. When we stopped at hotels, they would use towels and toilet paper to design clothes for their dolls or stuffed animals. Then they'd put their "babies" to bed in the drawers. It was so cute.

Through all the adventures we would often talk of the family history. The girls were shown the letters from their real grandfather and the pictures of Mary Lou. Chuck told them about his mother and the abuse of his stepfather. He also shared with Jen and Rebecca stories about the amazing people who helped shape him—Barb, the Jamesons, and the military. But the *unknown* of who his real father was was still there in our minds. The girls would ask questions about Chuck's family. More often than not, the answer was, "We don't know."

I'm not sure what sparked my action, but I became interested in seeing if I could find out anything more about Chuck's real father. I think having our own children gave me a desire for them to know their family history on both sides. So, when the girls were still in elementary school, I wrote to the Military Personnel

Records Center to see if there was any information. The response was a form letter stating that there had been a fire in St. Louis where many records were kept, and there was no way to get information. Dead end!

However, I think my sleuthing traits rubbed off on Rebecca. She had the Taylor name and knew the story of that name. When she was in middle school in 1990, she asked if she could write to the military for information on her grandfather Taylor. I told her, "Yes, please try!" So, she wrote in and received a similar form letter to mine—no records due to a fire. No luck. But the experience sparked Rebecca's interest in writing letters.

This was the era of the Gulf War, and many English classes were having students write letters to soldiers—no specific names or addresses, just to random soldiers. Most student letters went unanswered, but not Rebecca's. She received a letter from a Sgt. Dewey Taylor. What a surprise and a coincidence! She corresponded several times with him and told him her middle name and about her grandfather. He shared that he had a teenage daughter about her age and told her all about what he was seeing in the desert—the sand, the camels—we were all fascinated.

We now had letters from three different wars. From Charlie in World War II, stationed in the Pacific where he would write about the funny antics of the gooney birds. From Chuck who was stationed in Berlin and Vietnam and wrote about wanting to "wash this dirty war off." And now, from Dewey Taylor, stationed in Iraq and Kuwait, writing about the camels. We had just a small snapshot of military life and the different missions. All these letters and men had touched our family history in some way. But the secrets that emerged from Mary Lou's closet were stored in my heart, where they continued to gnaw at me.

I don't think I consciously looked for ways to honor our family; I feel that this desire is just a natural part of who I am. And setting the table for a gathering of friends or family is one of my favorite ways to honor those who are no longer with us. I love just about everything having to do with entertaining. As keeper of some of the family heirlooms, I use family celebrations as a time to showcase these treasures.

I have crystal water glasses and red glass sherbet goblets from my grandmother, whose name I have. The square etched-crystal dessert plates from my mom and dad are some of my favorites. I also use the silverware that I kept from Chuck's house. All of these pieces find a place at the table. It truly feels like all of the family members who once used them are there with us. Somewhere over the dinner talk, I point out the pieces and tell some of the history. Not sure if this comes from being the keeper of the family history, but it helps ground me.

As I reflect on our own family history, I recognize that glorious moments of love, laughter, and caring also had their share of heartache and pain. We navigated issues around my brother's divorce and my sister's verbal attacks on my parents. Our girls had typical sibling rivalries of jealousy and envy. There were broken bones, surgeries, and emotional upsets. Sometimes very angry words were shouted.

Occasionally, the girls would lose out at home when our professional lives became so demanding. Also, school was not always the happiest place for them, either. Some teachers who knew Chuck and me as administrators would be especially hard on our daughters. Chuck and I had to deal with politics in our jobs and with disappointments in our colleagues. We worked hard not to bring those issues home. We knew that our family needed to have a safe place to grow. He and I have been fortunate to have each other. We talked and made decisions about our life plans together. For me, I feel that life offers many "right answers." Chuck and I have been pretty intentional about embracing life.

During all of these years, the letters just sat in a box, gathering dust. We used them to give us some sense of who Charlie was. We imagined all kinds of scenarios—none of which was even *close* to what we were to discover in the years to come.

Jennifer Lee Eklund, b. May 1976 with baby sister, Rebecca Taylor Eklund, b. December 1977.

Jennifer and Rebecca Eklund. Family vacation at Hurricane Ridge in the Olympic Mountains, Washington State, c. 1981.

L to R: Aunt Valda (oldest), Marion (Ann's dad and only son in the family), Mary Cariker (Ann's mother and wife of Marion), Aunt Olyean (youngest), Aunt Bessie (second oldest). Cariker family reunion, East Texas, c. 1982.

7

Finding Mary Lou

Chuck had recollections of his mother sharing that she had been born and raised in South Bend, Indiana. Chuck knew that this was his hometown, too. South Bend is synonymous with the University of Notre Dame Fighting Irish and football. So it seemed natural that Chuck would be a Notre Dame (ND) fan. Through the years we would always cheer when Notre Dame played football. This only changed if ND was playing the University of Southern California—and then the USC Trojans had his allegiance. What was the root of these feelings of loyalty to a team? Was Mary Lou a Notre Dame fan? Charlie's last two letters say that he will be coming to see Mary Lou in the fall, and he offers to take her to a Notre Dame football game.

> *I envy you the opportunity of going to football games this fall. Here's a promise: If I return tin time, I'll take you to a Notre Dame game. Would you like that?*
>
> *Sept, 23, 1944*

Do they need an Army man to get the V-12's at Notre Dame in line? I'm a candidate. I love to push the Navy around. No comments! I'll bet you have been going out with the blooming Navy. Explain please.

Good bye darling until I see you.
Love,
Chas

3 October 1944

That visit from Charlie never happened. This was the last letter. The letters from their friend James Ballou seem to indicate that Mary Lou must have been told something that caused a breakup between Charlie and Mary Lou.

However, there were other connections to Notre Dame, too. Chuck had been sent to Catholic catechism as a child and Notre Dame was such an icon of the Catholic faith. When we cleaned out Mary Lou's house, we found rosary beads in her jewelry box, so we assumed that she'd been raised Catholic. Chuck also had been told that his mother had been excommunicated from the Catholic church because she married a divorced man. But that did not keep her from sending Chuck to catechism and dropping him off at mass on Sunday.

Visiting South Bend had never been in our plans. We just had these few strong connections to the place and a few pictures of Chuck as a toddler, all wrapped up in his hooded snowsuit walking down the sidewalk with piles of snow!

In the fall of the late 1980s, an unexpected opportunity arose. While I worked as a curriculum coordinator, I also did outside consulting with a big publisher of school textbooks. As a guest of the publishing company, I was invited to a national reading conference in South Bend at the University of Notre Dame. What a treat! An all-expenses-paid trip and visiting such a prestigious university.

I was so excited that I called Chuck at his school office, which I never did on a normal school day. But this was different. Could we financially pay for him to come with me to South Bend—his hometown? It was a chance in a lifetime. And with my parents' help taking care of our girls, we could make it happen.

Before I left for the conference, Chuck and I planned how we would spend our time—finding Mary Lou's old homes and seeing the streets where she had walked and played with her son. The letters from Charlie were key to our planning because Mary Lou had kept all of the letters in their *original envelopes*. The addresses where she had lived with little Chuck were spelled out for us. I carefully wrote them all down. We found maps of South Bend and Indiana at AAA. Would the houses that matched the addresses still be there?

In all the papers Mary Lou had saved, we also found her high school diploma—1932—from James Whitcomb Riley Senior High School. Would we be able to find it and visit? More ideas for visiting kept occurring to us because there is so much more to Indiana than South Bend.

Every year, as a young boy, Chuck listened to the Indianapolis 500 car race on the radio—and later, watched it on television. Every Sunday of the Memorial Day weekend, Chuck will be up early, listening and watching the introducing of the drivers, the conditions of the racetrack, the sounds of revving engines, the singing of "Back Home Again in Indiana." All of this would lead up to "Gentlemen, start your engines!" (Since now there are women drivers, the famous words are *"Drivers,* start your engines!") And off they go to cheering crowds.

Chuck would enjoy his morning coffee and be glued to the race until the final checkered flag and the drink of milk by the winner. If we were going to South Bend, could we see the Indy 500 track? Absolutely!

We also wanted to visit the capitol building in Indianapolis. As we studied maps and looked at travel suggestions, we discovered an Amish village in Ohio, not too far from South Bend. Could we fit this into our visit as well? Hopefully. We'd just have to wait and see how the trip would unfold.

Mary Lou Eklund with young son, Chuck (Charles Edward Taylor, Jr.).
Visit to the beach in Southern California, c. 1948.

The Ribbon Untied

Gustav Edvard Eklund with stepson, Chuck (Charles Edward Taylor, Jr.).
Visit to the beach in Southern California, c. 1948.

8

Visit to South Bend and Beyond

*F*or me, going to the conference and even staying in the dorms was a professional high. Being able to hear and see some of the top scholars in reading education felt like studying at the feet of greatness. It was inspiring to be on the University of Notre Dame campus with its ivy-covered walls and magnificent cathedral. I wasn't even Catholic, and I had a sense of some of Chuck's history. Had Mary Lou visited the campus as a girl growing up in South Bend? I would never know. But it was interesting to be in a place where she had blossomed as a young lady and where Chuck had been born and lived as a toddler.

Chuck joined me in a few days. I was so filled with information from the conference that I probably rattled on and on. But we were both ready to explore South Bend and find out what we could about where he had lived with his mother.

We stayed at a local motel, and even the motels were focused on Notre Dame football. Banners—green and gold, and sometimes blue and gold—were everywhere. We walked the beautiful tree-lined campus on paths that crisscrossed the university to the Grotto of Our Lady of Lourdes, into the cathedral, to the library, and of course, the student bookstore. There, we bought T-shirts and sweatshirts emblazoned with ND or "Fighting Irish." We found it interesting to notice street signs that gave directions for every day, and then different directions for "Game Day." We had never seen a town so wrapped up in the life of football! Maybe many small towns with an exceptionally well-known university and strong sports presence have a similar culture. We just soaked it all in while we talked about what his mother might have experienced growing up here.

As we ventured into South Bend, we found the Catholic hospital where Chuck had been born. Again, I imagined what his mother must have felt—alone? Was her sister there with her? What about her father? We knew these people were around because, once again, the letters from Charlie referenced them. We also drove through the grounds of Saint Mary's College because Charlie mentioned that Mary Lou was taking classes there.

Our next mission was to attempt to find the houses where Chuck and his mother had lived. The first house was still intact! We had the address, but we also had some photos of toddler Chuck walking on the sidewalk. In the background of one picture you see another large house. We were able to stand on the same spot from which the picture had been taken, hold up the photo, and see the same house. Yes—he really had lived here!

There were several other addresses, but all of these now were businesses. Still, finding that *one* was such a gift. As we explored, we realized that Mary Lou and young Chuck had moved around to several different places in those first few years of his life. I wondered again, how did she handle all of this?

Next, we found the high school from which Mary Lou had graduated, James Whitcomb Riley Senior High School. Since we were visiting in summer, there were no students and staff. We were both educators; we knew what the summer routines would be at a school. There would be lots of cleaning and very few people around. The school was a three-storied, yellowish brick or stone building that was magnificent to us. Coming from Southern California, we were used to school buildings being long and sprawling and open-aired. But in this part of the country, the typical school building was all enclosed.

We were able to get in and walk the halls. Silence, with just the whirring of the buffing machine. You could smell the wood floors and see the shine that was being put on them by the cleaning crew. The metal lockers were large and lined the halls. We walked by classrooms and journeyed deeper inside until we found the lead custodian. We shared who we were, and that Chuck's mother had gone to high school there. He was friendly and pleasant and told us that the school was going to be torn down in the next few years, and a new one built. He explained that it was more cost-effective to build a new school than to redesign the old one for the technology needs of the future.

It was sad to think that this lovely old building was coming down. But we were so glad to see it and imagine his mother's life as a teenager. The world was still enmeshed in the Great Depression then. How did this impact her life?

Visiting the high school and driving through the neighbor-hoods nearby gave us a sense of what life might have been like. Chuck and I both wished we could have had more time with Mary Lou and asked her about the stories of her life. Now we could only imagine. We spent a whole day exploring South Bend and walking in the neighborhoods where Mary Lou had lived.

The next day, we were off to Indianapolis and the Indy 500 track. If South Bend had the Notre Dame culture, then Indianapolis had the racing culture. Many of the businesses had signs and trinkets that advertised the main event—the big race. We were able to find our way to the track. Fortunately, they gave tours. Chuck was thrilled—me, not so much. However, it *was* wonderful to see him so excited, as he had watched the race for years, and I have heard his stories of the famous drivers in the history of the track.

The first race was in 1911—200 laps around an oval track. The only times the race had been called off were two years during World War I, and four years in World War II. Chuck knew it all! I have to admit that I was excited to ride around the track, even in a small tour bus—just not going 200+ miles per hour! And I could walk on the brick track and see the history of this great event. I found myself enjoying it all.

Back in our rental car, our next stop was the Indiana Statehouse, the state's capitol building. It was a warm, humid summer day, and we found a parking place near the building. Built in 1878, the capitol building is similar to the Washington capitol with its white stone, neoclassical architecture, and beautiful dome. The nine acres of park-like grounds included magnificent towering trees. We wandered around just absorbing the sights and sounds.

Again, our conversation would come back to wonderings about Mary Lou. Had she and her family visited the capitol? No way to know, but we gained some context for her life and the place she called home—and Chuck's home state.

We were almost finished with our visit when we made one last detour—to an Amish village in Ohio, just across the Indiana border. When we were early married, we had taken an American history class which included a visit to the Amish in the Pennsylvania Dutch Country. The people and history had fascinated us.

This adventure soon found us driving in *another era* . . . the horse-drawn buggies, the simple white clapboard houses, the clotheslines hung with drab-colored shirts and pants blowing in the breeze. The homes were surrounded by fields of corn soon ready for harvest—and no power lines went into the houses.

We approached a small town and pulled into an angled parking space. There were few cars, and the street was lined with one-story brick and wooden stores. We strolled along sidewalks with covered porches that blocked the glare of the hot sun. We passed no one and peeked through the windows. A drugstore caught our attention and we ventured inside.

Again, a step back in time. The store was still and quiet with only the whirring of overhead fans creating a cool retreat from the summer heat. It was a typical pharmacy with all the medicines and home remedies lining the shelves. Across the back of the store was a beautiful L-shaped marble-topped soda fountain with the clean empty glasses, the soda pumps, and all the flavors lined up along the back wall. Tall stools with leather-like upholstery were carefully spaced around the counter. Only one person was seated at the far end on the short side of the counter, an older gentleman in a plaid shirt with his straw hat lying on the stool next to him.

We sat down at the counter and looked around. We were greeted by a waitress who smiled and asked what we would like to

The Ribbon Untied

have. Almost in a whisper, we ordered malts—chocolate for Chuck and vanilla for me. Just like in times from our childhood, our malts came in tall frosted glasses with swirled whipped cream and a bright red cherry on top. And, of course, the red-striped straw and long spoon. What could be better!

As we sipped our malts, it wasn't long before we caught the eye of the man sitting at the counter and began to chat. He wanted to know, "Where are you from? What brings you here?" We weren't shy about sharing our story and asking questions about the town and some of the Amish ways. The gentleman explained that he was a driver for the Amish girls who worked at a bakery a few streets over. The Amish don't use gas-powered transportation, so he was hired to drive the girls to work, wait for them to complete their shift, and then drive them home.

As we chatted, our waitress joined the conversation. We had assumed that she was not Amish since she didn't wear the long, aproned dress and bonnet-type cap. We were very surprised when she openly told us that she'd been raised Amish but had married outside the Amish faith. She had been shunned and could no longer have any contact with her family. She told us how difficult that was. But she had made that choice. And she hoped that someday they would be able to see each other again.

We finished our malts and said our good-byes. As we walked outside, we could see three or four horse-drawn buggies at the end of the street and a group of Amish men, bearded and in hats and dark clothes. It appeared that one of them had a new horse and was showing it off. They were lifting up the horse's lips and checking its teeth. As Chuck said, "Just like someone showing off a new car and kicking the tires!" They paid no mind to us.

As we were returning to our car, we saw an incredible sight in the distance. Through the cornfields, we spied a horse-drawn wagon with two Amish teenagers aboard, racing through the field! The light was beautiful as it captured the colors of a late summer afternoon and the feeling of the delight of youth, traveling in a different time.

Our day couldn't have been more perfect—from the race-track for fast-paced machines in the morning to that wagon flying across the cornfields in the afternoon. All these adventures brought us just a bit closer to Mary Lou and some of Chuck's roots.

Mary Louise Haines. Graduation picture from James Whitcomb Riley Senior High School, South Bend, Indiana, c. 1932.

9

Finding Peggy

*O*ver the next twenty years, our visit to South Bend and surrounding Indiana stayed in our memories. We made the assumption that Charlie had died in World War II, and that was that. Occasionally, often over the last of the dinner wine, Chuck and I would think of that visit and wonder about all of the what-ifs. Why had Mary Lou left South Bend? What would his life—and our lives—have been like if . . .

The what-ifs were just a game. We were busy living our lives. Chuck and I had successful careers in education as teachers and then school administrators: Chuck as a high school principal and I as an elementary school principal. Both of these professional steps led us to serve as directors at a school-district level. Fortunately, we were in different districts, just neighborhood cities apart, so local politics and competition between the school districts could be left at the door of our home. Chuck supervised secondary principals for ten years before retiring in 2006, after thirty-four years in education. I supervised elementary school

96   The Ribbon Untied

principals for six years before retiring in 2007, with thirty-nine years under my belt!

Chuck took to retirement like a duck to water. Retirement had not necessarily been on my agenda until I saw how much Chuck was enjoying the lack of political stress and his newfound freedom to do as he pleased. As I thought about retirement, I wasn't sure I was ready. I needed to have *something to go to*—a direction.

Seeking new directions, I began to work with a life coach. She and I held all of our discussions on early morning calls as I laid out my ideas, fears, and excitement about the possibilities of retirement. I was so sure I needed to go to *something*—open a business, do consulting—not just be another volunteer with all of the old retired persons!

She had me completing interest surveys and pulling pictures from magazines about creative job possibilities. I designed charts about what my strengths were and what people would say about my talents. Being a dutiful student, I completed all of my assignments. I am one who is often reflective, and I was enjoying the process. However, none of these exercises made me feel that I was moving any closer to a decision. I was just wandering around with retirement possibilities floating in my head. I hadn't told anyone but Chuck that I was contemplating retirement, so I just carried on in my job—busy and wondering.

In February of 2007, Chuck and I took a short trip on a long weekend to meet some friends in Sedona, Arizona. The scenery was like nothing I'd ever seen before. The stark red rock formations and big-sky vistas seemed to speak to my soul in a primitive way. The weather was cold and often a bit snowy, which seemed to add to the mystery of the red rocks as flakes of snow softly floated around these giant structures.

On one of our adventures, we went to Cathedral Rock to visit a small chapel. The snow fluttered down gently, and the sky was gray. As we entered the small chapel, there was soft Gregorian chant music playing and dim light from outside pouring in, highlighting the few pews. There was a quiet peacefulness, and red candles lined both sides of the wall leading up to the altar. The front end of the chapel was built into the side of the red rocks, and the altar was all glass, looking out over the red rocks in the valley.

I found myself drawn to the front of the altar and stood there, gazing out at the view. What caught my eye was the reflection of the red candles that were behind me. Amazingly, this reflection extended the light of the candles through the glass wall and *into the snow-covered rocks outside*. I slowly turned and stared at the candles burning behind me. Then I slowly turned back to face the altar and followed the line of light moving forward into the snow—a bit blurred, but still reflecting the burning candles.

Without even knowing what hit me, I realized, as I looked at the burning candles behind me, that they symbolized the professional life I had accomplished. What I needed to do was to let go and trust that more red candles would appear when the time was right. I didn't need to have a plan. I just needed to have faith and trust that new candles would come my way, and that I could choose to light them whenever I wanted to.

I knew in that moment that I was ready to retire. It couldn't have been clearer; there would be no second-guessing. It was like a huge weight had been lifted from me.

Slowly walking to the back of the chapel, I found Chuck. Through tears streaming down my face, I told him I was ready to retire.

I'm guessing that Chuck wasn't surprised. He just smiled his calm smile and gave me a gentle kiss. He knows me well and could probably see it coming.

A few weeks later, our friends with whom we had traveled to Sedona were over for dinner. Over our dessert and last sips of wine, Chuck surprised me with a picture that captured me standing at the front of that altar in the chapel as I was having my epiphany. He had made the photo into a large print and framed it! Along with the picture was a magnificent silver "Navajo pearl" necklace. I had eyed this beauty on one of the many Sedona shopping stops. With the help of these dear friends Chuck had managed to secretly purchase it. It was an evening I will never forget, with my most loving husband and thoughtful friends.

Over the next few weeks at work, I began the process of sharing that I was retiring. I used the picture to tell my colleagues about my decision and, of course, wore my Navajo pearls often. I call this life episode the "red candle" moment. Ever since then, I have used "red candles" as a metaphor for continuing my life adventures—into retirement and new possibilities.

When I see something that is a red candle moment, I stop and pay close attention to my world around me. In the last few years there have been many red candles. I admire the "glassybaby" candle that sits on the sill of our kitchen window, and I'm constantly reminded that there are more red candle moments to come if I am patient and watch carefully.

As I retired and made myself more open to a lack of structure and being okay with no plan for the day, I found I was being drawn to exploring more about family history—mine and Chuck's.

About this same time, ancestry.com was becoming a thing. The news and advertisements for locating your family were all around. I became fascinated. I certainly had the time to play at the computer and see what I could discover.

My parents had both passed away; my father in 2001 (at ninety-three) and my mother in 2004 (at ninety-two). They had both been keepers of the family history. They had organized letters and pictures, and all of these artifacts had been given to me. My brother and sister didn't seem to have the same interest, so I had time and technology on my side. I could hunt and delve into the past to my heart's content. As I look back at this time, it's obvious to me that all these elements—time, resources, and passion—came together to form a red candle moment.

For hours I would sit in my cozy home office at the computer, surrounded by favorite books, pictures, and "stuff" from my professional life. And I learned to sleuth!

Beginning to use ancestry.com was my first attempt at using databases with so much information. The most valuable tools for locating someone were the census records, which provided decades of information about who lived where and with whom. The census is taken every ten years and shows all persons and the state in which they were born. The persons in each household—in small villages, towns, and cities across our country—are counted.

To search the data in these records I needed to start with some basic information about the person. Plugging in their first, middle, and last name and birthday would lead me to a match. The technology was a bit scary to me, but I wasn't working for anyone but myself, so I could make mistakes and learn as I was discovering the past. Fortunately, the software that ancestry.com used would often give me prompts that aided me in my search.

I started with the census records and names of my own family members. Since I knew these names and birth dates, I was able to have success quickly. It was fascinating to find my grandparents. I could see their faces in my mind as their names popped up on the screen—Cariker and Rush—in the 1890 and 1900 census, and then to see in 1910, there was my father, born in 1908! I repeated these steps with the names on my mother's side—Kennedy and Page—and in the 1920 census, there was my mother, born in 1912.

As I became more comfortable with ancestry.com, I noodled around and found other databases: deaths, marriages, births. On the census records I could see where each of these families was located and if others lived with them or on the same property. Sometimes I would find a name of someone—not a family member, maybe a boarder. I could also see who lived on the same road, lane, or street. Powerful tools!

With all of this information, the lives of my ancestors became more real. My father often told the story of his father learning to drive a Model A while my grandmother sat next to him, reading the instruction booklet out loud. Just maybe this event happened at one of these addresses I was discovering from the census. Over many family gatherings we would laugh at this story as we imagined my somewhat domineering grandmother and my mild-mannered grandfather *driving around in circles* until she reached the section in the "how-to" booklet on how to stop!

Finding all of these names created a sense of wholeness to my family. The roots were deep, and even if some of the family stories were not exactly accurate, they conveyed a feeling of lives well lived. It was a gift to have family roots. Since I know my roots, it's hard to imagine not knowing them, but Chuck knew only bits and pieces of his. Could I help find more pieces of his family? Could we find more family stories to weave into his life? At what cost? And what benefit?

From my upstairs office window, I had a view of a redbud tree that grew between our house and the very close neighbor's house. And through the seasons I would watch the buds appear—pinkish red—and then the small-pointed leaves would appear and go from light green to darker as the summer approached. When the cooler season arrived, the leaves would slowly turn to dark orange and fall to the ground or be blown away in the fierce Santa Ana winds of Southern California.

My family tree just kept growing as I found more and more information. But unlike the tree outside my window, the leaves on this tree had more staying power—or maybe each family member leaf would eventually blow away and the circle of life would start again. It is interesting to think about trees being a symbol for keeping the ancestors organized.

All of my playing and reflecting on family history on ancestry.com was filling my time. It was fun to share my discoveries with Chuck and our girls. So naturally, I began to branch out—no pun intended.

Here we are in 2008, both of us retired and still wondering about Chuck's family. Could I find out *anything* about the roots of his family tree? We had a few clues. Chuck knew his mother's maiden name, Haines, and he knew he was from South Bend, Indiana. He had some recollection that his mother had told him he had an aunt and a grandfather still in Indiana. Taking these bits of information, I began to search for the Haines family leaves.

And there they were. Again, for census records, names and birthdays were a key. I backtracked in the census records from 1930 to 1920 to 1910 to 1900. I was able to find Chuck's grandfather, Wilson David Haines, born April 7, 1871, and Chuck's grandmother, Pearl Ivy Haines, born in 1879. These records also

The Ribbon Untied

indicated that his grandmother, Pearl, had been born in Germany and spoke German. The records also showed Chuck's aunt, Evelyn, and his mother, Mary Lou. Just like when I found my family and their location, I was able to see the address where Mary Lou had lived with her family.

The mysteries persisted and my curiosity was piqued! What else could I find?

My sleuthing continued and I plugged in names, dates, and possible places the Haines family had lived. I discovered that the marriage and obituary files were the most useful. Since marriages and deaths have to be recorded in state databases, there are many statistics available. Having found Wilson and Pearl Haines in the 1930 census, I was able to move forward and find the dates of their marriage and deaths. Then, plugging in the name Evelyn Haines, I found that Chuck's aunt had married Walter Barrett, and I found their children's names in the census. These were *Chuck's cousins*—Marilyn, Lois, Walter (Bud), Peggy, and James.

Again, once I found this information, the questions came. Why had Mary Lou left Indiana? Why didn't Chuck know or have any contact with these relatives?

I knew all my aunts and uncles and cousins. We had sleep-overs at our grandparents' house. We shared holidays and summer vacations. Chuck had none of this. It seems like having family ties can help define you, and maybe not having family ties defines you, too.

Now Chuck was becoming more curious. Who were these people? Did they know anything about his mother and him?

My quest to find some answers continued. One of the things I discovered about ancestry.com was the need to be persistent and to look at solving a problem from lots of angles. On more than one occasion I'd hit a roadblock—after all, Haines was a relatively common name. I would try plugging in different dates or places. Sometimes I would get so frustrated with my lack of success that I'd just walk away from the computer for several days. But then I would get a new idea or think of a new way to approach gathering information and try again. The power of positive reinforcement played a part in my continuing. I would find one clue or add one leaf to the growing data, and my power to sleuth would be renewed.

In this process I finally put in all the cousins' names and found that Marilyn, the oldest cousin, had married and had three children. As I searched further, I found an obituary of her death—and there, right in front of me on the computer screen, were all of the histories of the cousins! I could see who had died and who was still alive with spouses. It was like winning Bingo. Not every person who dies has this detailed an obituary, but Marilyn did.

This brief, detailed write-up gave me clues to keep me going again, and I was off and running! Now, having some skills with ancestry.com, I was able to locate the Haines cousins. Here were Peg and her husband, John, and James and his wife, Vivian. Both of them lived in the same town. This discovery led to my getting acquainted with finding names online. The phone book and yellow page listings of years past are now online. These people locator information sites have more information than the old phone books did. I did find myself feeling somewhat guilty about looking up these names; it felt like I was spying. *They* didn't know anyone was looking for them, and if I chose to pay a fee for additional information, I could find out if they had been in jail. That would have been going too far. The home addresses were the keys to contacting them.

Chuck and I had interesting discussions about how and if we should try to make contact. What if they didn't want to acknowledge him? How would he feel if they wouldn't accept his offer to know them? What could they tell us? Could we arrange to meet them?

The excitement of finding family members far outweighed the possibility of rejection. Because I had such wonderful family memories of cousins, I needed to be aware that my experiences could be pushing Chuck to take the next steps. Maybe all wouldn't be as exciting as I imagined. After much thought, Chuck wrote a letter to Peggy. He introduced himself and included his phone number.

When you put yourself out there, wherever "there" is, the anticipation of consequences can be exciting and a bit stressful. I was encouraging Chuck on this journey of family finding. But I knew that it could come back to cause more pain. Sending this letter somehow seemed different than sitting on the floor and calling Dr. Ballou about his brother. That had been a lark or an impulsive action. This seemed so much more real. We now had verified actual evidence of family members and real addresses.

I don't remember how many days passed before we had word from Chuck's cousin. He had also sent the same letter to the youngest cousin, James. We had no idea if we would ever hear from anyone. After several weeks, the phone call from Peggy came with a warm hello! I was relieved and very excited to have my sleuthing pay off.

The phone call was just the beginning. I recall the excitement in Chuck's voice as he and Peggy talked. He gave a general explanation about how we found them through the obituary of the oldest cousin, Marilyn. Peggy told Chuck that the family never knew where Mary Lou had moved to. Hearing that we were in California was news to her. Chuck explained where we lived and that we were retired now. Over the course of the conversation, Chuck and Peggy made arrangements for us to come and visit them. Peggy and her husband, John, were now in their late seventies. They were in the process of moving into a retirement village. It was decided that we would meet them for lunch in a local restaurant in Mishawaka, Indiana, which was very close to South Bend. The date of July 27, 2009, was set, and now we could figure out how.

Between me and Chuck, I don't know who was more excited. Chuck had heard from a cousin whom he had never known, and we were going to see her and her husband in his home state! Maybe in my mind I could envision tiny roots of a family tree beginning to grow.

Baby Chuck (Charles Edward Taylor, Jr.), 1944.

Chuck (Charles Edward Taylor, Jr.). Enjoying the snow outside his home in South Bend, Indiana, c. 1945.

The Ribbon Untied

10

"Back Home Again in Indiana"

*N*ow that we'd made the date with Peggy, we got into high gear to plan the trip!

This trip came with many unexpected and pleasant surprises. We were putting two missions together. Our oldest daughter Jen and her significant other (soon-to-be husband), Jeff, were leaving Ann Arbor, Michigan, after her postdoctoral work. She was taking a teaching position at Western State College of Colorado in Gunnison. She and Jeff needed our help in taking two cars, two cats, and many of their belongings from Michigan to Colorado.

Chuck and I were up for the trip, and we would combine this adventure with going to meet Cousin Peggy in Indiana. It would be a circuitous route with us driving our car from California to the airport in Denver. There, we'd leave our car and hop on a plane to South Bend, renting a car there to meet Peggy. From South Bend we would fly to Detroit to meet Jen and Jeff. Then two couples in two cars would drive across the country in tandem to Colorado. Last, Chuck and I would drive home to California. That was the plan.

In the midst of heading east on this whirlwind trip, we came to meet Peggy!

The morning of our luncheon date with her, Chuck and I took the time to retrace some of our steps from our earlier trip to South Bend in the late 1980s. This time we had the actual address of the Haines homestead on E. Donald. The research on ancestry.com was paying off.

The large two-story house sat on a corner lot. The front porch with two pillars seemed small for the size of the house. But as we looked at the footprint, it appeared that there were several additions and apartment-type structures that had been added along the side. It was difficult to see the house's original size and shape. There were a few other houses of similar vintage around the neighborhood, but right across the street was a used car lot with flags waving from light post to light post. It was interesting for us to see it now and imagine what life could have been like for Mary Lou and her family back in the 1920s and '30s. There certainly wouldn't have been a used car lot, but there would be other big two-storied, clapboard houses on a tree-lined street. On this visit in 2009, there were only a few houses that seemed to have been turned into apartments. Now the neighborhood is on the edge of more businesses, and the streets are filled with cars.

A few blocks away from the homestead, we drove past the new high school that had replaced the one we had visited in the 1980s. The new structure was built with the similar brick and yellowish stone. Again, wondering if Mary Lou and friends had walked to school and what life was like in the early 1930s. The Great Depression was taking its toll across the country then. But interestingly, I don't remember my parents (similar in age to Mary Lou) talking too much about their life during that time. What did teenagers do?

We also revisited the houses where Chuck had lived. Once again, we found the house where he had played on the sidewalk. This time we were armed with a camera and took pictures. The house was being renovated, and an old toilet was sitting on the stoop of the front porch. The construction crew was in the house, and we boldly asked if we could come in and look around. No problem for them.

Chuck and I wandered through the house. Mary Lou and Chuck had lived in a side apartment that had an entrance with a small porch. With everything being gutted for remodeling, it was difficult to get any sense of how it had been arranged, but just seeing the house gave us an idea of where Chuck had spent his very early years.

Chuck posed for a picture in the same spot on the sidewalk where his mother had taken his picture as a toddler. The same neighboring house can be seen in the background in all of the toddler pictures, which covered the seasons—Chuck in short pants on a very small tricycle or push toy; in overalls and a short-sleeved shirt, holding a ball; one in shorts; and Chuck in the snowsuit with snow piled high.

There was also a picture of another child, wearing a fireman's hat and riding a larger tricycle on the sidewalk. Chuck is off to the side squatting down and petting a small dog. You can almost hear him laughing with glee as it seems the puppy is licking him. Chuck recalls his mother telling him that he had a friend that they called "Little Joe from Kokomo." We have often wondered if this picture is of Little Joe.

As I look back at these pictures of Chuck as a happy child and see the house, the street, and the neighborhood, I think about the possibility of *happy moments for Mary Lou*. She made an effort to

The Ribbon Untied

take his picture through the seasons and show his childhood joy. She kept all of these pictures in the shoebox with the letters from Charlie—but never chose to share them with her son.

When we travel somewhere new, Chuck and I often leave ourselves extra time, and this trip was no exception. On our way to meet Cousin Peggy and John at the café, we had a bit of time to waste and decided to visit a shopping mall. We had noticed darkening skies, and as we were parking, a wild midwestern rainstorm came roaring through. We stepped from the car and immediately felt the difference in the air. It brought back memories of this type of storm from my childhood in southeast Texas—and I always enjoyed crazy weather. As is so typical, the temperature drops slightly, and the skies quickly become blackish gray. The wind comes up and the heavens seem to open and pour buckets of water! These quick summer storms usually last a few minutes before moving on. Then, bright sunshine appears and the hot sticky humidity returns.

Through the deluge we ran across the parking lot and into the mall. No sooner were we inside than the storm was over. We were a bit soggy and giggled about being wet like two little kids. But our summer clothes dried quickly as the cool air-conditioning chilled us.

Over the next half hour or so we wandered the mall. Our meandering was a bit of a diversion because I think both of us were anxious about meeting Peggy and John. Chuck and Peggy hadn't gone into too much detail about his early years when they had talked on the phone. So we had many questions waiting to be asked. Some of these may not find answers and just remain as wonderings . . .

Again, we arrived a few minutes early to check out our surroundings. We had often noticed that the restaurants or diners in small towns are meeting places for local groups, with signs taped on their windows like "Rotary Club meeting on Mondays." This diner was no different. It was a bit more upscale than a Denny's and had all of the decorations that are so common to this type of restaurant. There is always the small wooden bench and a few wooden chairs in the entrance next to the check-in counter. The tall, refrigerated cake display is filled with homemade pies and cakes, inviting drooling and thinking about dessert. Then the big open room with booths around the perimeter and tables in the middle. The booths and benches are covered in Naugahyde. The faux-wood paneling, wallpaper, and big windows that look out over flower boxes complete the décor.

All of the tables were laminated. As if standing at attention, all of the condiments were lined up against the end of the table. And there was the distinctive smell permeating the air of many years' worth of meals that have been deep-fried or cooked on a grill. In the summer heat there was the icy air-conditioning that reminds me of the odors inside a refrigerator filled with leftovers. The floors were indoor/outdoor carpet. Everything was clean, neat, and shiny, ready for serving guests. The setting was familiar, but the circumstances were unlike any we had known.

We were waiting to meet Chuck's cousin whom he didn't even know he had until just a few months ago. And now he was seeing her, knowing that she had been a part of his very early childhood that he didn't remember.

Chuck and I, for all outward appearances, sat calmly and quietly on the wooden bench waiting for Peggy and John. I am sure we were both deep in thought about what the next few hours would bring. What would Peggy and John look like? What would they say? What would we learn about Mary Lou?

Right on time, Peggy and John walked through the door. Peggy smiled and said, "I would recognize you anywhere!" and gave Chuck a big hug. Chuck with his white hair at age sixty-five and his arms wrapped around Peggy with her colored hair in her late seventies—it was a beautiful sight, a special moment. The old saying is "Long lost cousins . . ." Well, these cousins had finally found each other.

We exchanged friendly hellos and introductions and then moved to a table in a far corner.

After we were seated, I observed that Peggy had a softness about her that was comforting. She wore her brownish-red hair in tight curls that framed her gentle face. She looked like many women in their seventies, slightly rounded and working at keeping herself healthy. She was dressed in a comfortable white shirt with black-and-white checked trim at the neck and sleeves and black pull-on pants. John also had a kind face and curly gray hair. He was dressed in a blue short-sleeved shirt and slacks. They could have been my parents—ordinary people living their lives.

Our waitress came. Again, the typical diner menu options of salads, sandwiches, burgers, sodas, and iced tea. I'm not sure what we ordered. I can't even remember eating, but soon the table was cleared.

I felt like a baby bird that waits for its mother to return to the nest to feed her babies. I was just waiting for that morsel! But this was about Chuck and Peggy. John and I were the bystanders watching this meeting unfold.

Peggy slowly unzipped and carefully laid out a beautiful pink-flowered, soft-clothed briefcase that was filled with picture books and envelopes of pictures. There were so many questions on our part! Where does the conversation start? Peggy was the keeper of much of the family history. Her mother, Evelyn, had been six years older than Mary Lou.

Peggy seemed very comfortable sharing about her recollections from the point of view of a girl going into her teenage years. That was when she had known her Aunt Mary Lou and little Charlie. Peggy's family had called Chuck "Charlie." Chuck and I sat and listened without asking questions. There didn't seem to be any order to the memories, just an outpouring of her thoughts. She would share pictures from her albums as she told us about her life. Since she and John were moving into the retirement home, she had been going through family albums and had a quick knowledge of where to find things. She shared pictures of the cousins as she talked about her four siblings. She was next to the youngest. Her older siblings, Marilyn, Lois, and Walter, had already passed away. Even though Chuck didn't know these cousins, this was an endearing way for him to learn about them.

After Peggy had shared about her childhood family, she began to talk about Mary Lou.

Peggy told us, "I was about eleven years old when Charlie was born. Around that time, my youngest brother James was also born, and the two of them became playmates."

I may not have all of the memories exact, and Chuck does not remember this, but I seem to recall that Peggy said Grandfather Haines lived with her family—with Evelyn and Walter and the five children. This extended family would have been the norm, and Mary Lou and Charlie would have seen him often.

She recalled, "Aunt Mary Lou would bring you over to our house, and you and my brother would sit side by side in highchairs." She shared a picture of the two toddlers in their highchairs and chuckled at the memory of how cute they were together!

Peggy said that the family still has the highchair and that it has been used by other second cousins and grandchildren. I think Peggy enjoyed being the big sister who took on the babysitting role for her little brother and cousin Charlie.

Peggy shared more memories. "Mary Lou was glamorous, and she smelled so good!" Peggy didn't elaborate on what she meant by glamorous, but from a young teenager's mind, I am guessing that Mary Lou had beautiful clothes, wore makeup, and used perfume. Maybe these were things her own mother did not do—after all, Peggy's mom had five children and was taking care of her sister's child on occasion.

She said, "When Aunt Mary Lou would come for a visit with little you, she had a suitcase that she'd place on the bed. I would stand at the door and watch her open it. There was always a picture of a man on the top." At this point in the conversation, Chuck pulled out the leather photo frame with the picture of the man we thought was Chuck's father. That picture had been in the shoebox with the letters.

He asked, "Could this have been the picture?" She wasn't sure, but it fit with the memory.

Peggy said, "A point that caused the greatest concern in the family was what seemed a lack of responsibility by Mary Lou . . . to be the most responsible mother. Your mother would leave you with us for a few days and take off. My mother, your Aunt Evelyn, would call Mary Lou to come pick you up. We weren't sure where Mary Lou went, but that caused the family to be concerned."

She said, "There was friction between my mother (Evelyn) and Aunt Mary Lou and probably Grandpa Haines. All of us kids knew that Mary Lou was leaving and taking you with her. We four oldest cousins tried to convince our father to *keep you.*

We seemed to feel that you were part of the family. I was ten years older than the youngest. Maybe we felt this would be a good situation for baby James. Charlie and James could grow up like brothers."

Peggy went on to say, "The family often wondered where the two of you went. But it wasn't until the mid-1970s that someone— I can't recall who—had read an obituary about the death of your mother and contacted my mom." That was the only information they ever had about Mary Lou's whereabouts. But, Peggy said, "In my family, we often talked about where you and your mother might have gone."

It felt like we were drinking from a firehose—so much information was gushing out! Chuck and I just listened. Slowly, Chuck began to share the few pictures of himself in front of the house in South Bend and to ask some questions about being Catholic. No, Peggy said, they were not Catholic. Chuck went on to tell about finding the rosary beads in his mother's jewelry box and that he'd been sent to catechism as a boy. Peggy assured us that they were not Catholic, but that she had married a Catholic (nodding to John) and she herself had converted to Catholicism. So where and when did his mother decide to become a Catholic?

Then Chuck asked about his grandfather. He thought he remembered his mother saying that his grandfather was an engineer and maybe even taught at a university. Again, no. Grandpa Haines was a road engineer and drove big equipment. Chuck then told them that as a little boy he had been taught the fight song from Georgia Tech: "I'm a Ramblin' Wreck from Georgia Tech and a hell of an engineer—" So where had that all come from? We wondered together, but Peggy didn't have any insights into this story.

As lunch drew to a close, Chuck and Peggy promised to stay in touch. She said she would send more pictures of his grandfather and his aunt—her mother. Fortunately, Peggy was a keeper of family history and she shared so graciously with us! I felt that Peggy was bringing closure to a part of her life and was happy that the baby cousin she had loved and cared for had made it in the world. She had played a part in Chuck's young life.

Peggy and John were at a new point in their long lives, and maybe this reunion brought wholeness to her family. We all hugged and said our good-byes, and Chuck and I walked away with our hearts and minds full.

Chuck and I often need time, hours or days, to process information before we start unraveling the details. As we drove along the country roads from Mishawaka to South Bend, we quietly marveled at all of the new "pieces" of Mary Lou. Many "facts" we thought we knew were turned upside down. Maybe Mary Lou wasn't a Catholic, and Chuck's grandfather wasn't a teacher at Georgia Tech. More questions . . . but we also came away with some new roots of the family tree—learning about Chuck's early childhood from the insights of an older cousin.

The next day we were heading out to Ann Arbor, Michigan, to meet our daughter and future son-in-law to help them move. There would be many hours to drive and talk and revisit what we had heard. We would also be able to tell Jen and Jeff about meeting Peggy and the new information she'd given us.

As we caravanned with our kids across the plains of Iowa and Nebraska and into Colorado, Chuck and I wondered about the train trip that had carried Mary Lou and her son from South Bend to California. One of Chuck's earliest memories was about the train tracks. He would have been less than three years old, so this was an extraordinary event to make such a memory.

When I hear Chuck tell of this memory, I am always struck with the strength that Mary Lou had to pick up her life and start anew with her son in a new place with no family support. She was a single mom, educated with a nursing degree; she had served in the Army Nurses Corps and had witnessed and was involved in the bombing of Pearl Harbor. Many women in that period of history were stepping forward, as symbolized by the iconic Rosie the Riveter. Mary Lou was stepping forward into a different world, too, and taking her young son with her. I am sure there was pain and sorrow, but perhaps she had an inner resolve to do it her way.

Finding and meeting Peggy and John was a gift. It came unexpectedly and with many surprises. There was joy in discovering more about my mother-in-law, and now I had even more questions.

Getting home to the comfort of my office, the computer, and ancestry.com became even more inviting. What else could I discover?

L to R: John Hess and Peggy Hess. Lunch meeting with Cousin Peggy and her husband. Mishawaka, Indiana, 2008.

Mary Lou Haines and young son, Chuck (Charles Edward Taylor, Jr.). Enjoying the park in South Bend, Indiana, c. 1945-46. This photo was given to Chuck by his cousin Peggy in 2008.

The Ribbon Untied

This is the apartment house where Mary Lou and son, Chuck (Charles Edward Taylor, Jr.), lived in South Bend, Indiana, c. 1944-45. Picture taken in 2008 on our trip to Indiana to meet Cousin Peggy. The house was located using the addresses on the envelopes sent to Mary Lou by Charles Taylor.

Newspaper obituary of Wilson David Haines (Chuck's grandfather). This small document, given to us by Cousin Peggy, provided valuable information about Mary Lou's mother's maiden name, Pearl Shock. 1955.

Wilson David Haines

Wilson David Haines, 84, R. R. 4, Plymouth, passed away at 6 p. m. Friday at Parkview hospital after a three month illness. He was born April 7, 1871 in Whitley county to Benjamin and Margaret Haines. His wife, Pearl Shock Haines, preceded him in death in 1931. Mr Haines was a construction worker.

Survivors include two daughters, Mrs. Evelyn Barrett of Plymouth. and Miss Mary Louise Haines of Los Angeles, Calif; six grandchildren and five great-grandchildren.

Friends may call at the Danielson and VanGilder Funeral Home where services will be held at 10 a.m. Monday. Rev. Leo Erny will officiate and interment will be in Glenwood cemetery at Roanoke.

The Ribbon Untied

11

Finding Charlie

*J*igsaw puzzles have always interested me. The box comes with all of those little pieces, each one adding to the whole. On the outside of the box is the picture of what it will be when all the pieces are joined together. The picture offers a road map for the completed project.

My method for "doing a jigsaw" is to start by completing the border with the straight edges, and then move to pieces that are the most recognizable—a horse's leg, a steeple, the horizon, a building, or a special landscape feature. Once the familiar scenes are in place, the surrounding details are added. Searching for ancestors can be like putting a jigsaw puzzle together.

As I began seeking to discover my ancestors, I started with border pieces: names of people or places I recognized and knew to be true. My own family history had many recognizable markers, or facts I knew about the lives of those who lived before me. I could see the whole picture—not the details of their lives but the big picture, much like what is on the box top. I had the vantage point of knowing the big pieces and then adding some of my own personal experiences or details.

However, Chuck's family puzzle pieces proved to be very challenging. To begin with, there were few places to start—the letters in the shoebox and Chuck's recollections—but not many big markers on which to build.

Finding Cousin Peggy was an important event that added larger pieces to the puzzle. Peggy was good on her word and sent additional pictures. We now had pictures of Grandpa Haines and Aunt Evelyn.

She also included a few more pictures of Chuck and his mother together. One of my favorites is of Mary Lou sitting on a swing holding toddler Charlie. With big smiles, they posed for the camera, both dressed in sandals and shorts. They seemed happy and carefree on a summer afternoon. I can imagine that Mary Lou and Charlie had gone to the park with Aunt Evelyn and the cousins. The looks on their faces seem to capture a joyful, loving moment between a mother and child. On the back of the photo was written: "Aunt Mary and Chuckie." Was this how Peggy and her siblings remembered them?

Other than the pictures, there was no further contact between Peggy and Chuck. I have wondered about this. Was it enough for Chuck just to know about his grandfather, aunt, and cousins? Did Peggy feel any need to stay in touch now that the mystery of Mary Lou and Charlie's whereabouts was solved? Maybe the puzzle pieces were really more of a collage—people, places, and events loosely hung together that have meaning as I look at the whole, but individually not as significant.

Our adventure to meet Cousin Peggy and John was soon becoming a distant memory. Peggy's recounting her experience of her Aunt Mary Lou as a young teenager was a new point of view. Maybe in the future, second or third cousins on the Mary Lou Haines side of the family might search for family history. But for now, Chuck had no continuing relationships with anyone on his mother's side of the family. They were related in name only.

After that visit to South Bend, we quickly became busy with everyday life events that took our time and enriched our lives. That summer of 2008 after meeting Peggy, I had been invited to work part time at a California state university in the School of Education. In this new role I supervised student teachers. Then over the course of several months, I was offered a position as a lecturer and teacher for several sections of students entering the teaching profession. This energized me. Working with young people who were preparing to become teachers was a dream job! This was truly a red candle moment in my life.

Because of these time commitments, I wasn't able to jump back into the family research. But as I became more familiar with the ins and outs of university life, I was able to adjust my schedule to give me some time to explore Chuck's family history.

Where would I find puzzle pieces now? I still had this burning desire to find out about Chuck's real father.

To be able to maximize the data on ancestry.com, I realized I needed a few more key facts, names, and dates from the Taylor side. Chuck's original birth certificate gave his name as Charles Edward Taylor, Jr. The Taylor name could be a *big* puzzle piece. Being a junior implied there was a *senior* Charles Edward Taylor.

I plugged in Charles Edward Taylor, Sr. over and over again. I never realized how many Charles Edward Taylors there are in the United States; the census records indicated hundreds! I needed to have a plan to filter the data. Looking for data clues took me back to the letters from Charlie to Mary Lou. This was really all I had.

For days I pored over the letters. I took each letter in chronological order and made lists of what I thought were significant points.

Since we had met Cousin Peggy and heard her stories, the letters from Charlie Senior had renewed significance. And there were indications in these letters that all may not have been well with her family in the years past.

> *I'm also glad that you have been seeing your father and that things are working out to your satisfaction even tho' the Maine trip was postponed.*
>
> *3 September 1944*

> *What does your sister and Dad think of young slug? Does he pass inspection? (Not the Army kind yet, I hope.)*
>
> *3 October 1944*

These are quotes from the last two of the nineteen letters that Charlie sent to Mary Lou. He never directly acknowledges that Charlie is his son, but he asks about him and asks for pictures. Mary Lou would have been receiving these letters while she was still in South Bend. Comments made in the letters indicate that Mary Lou had shared her concerns about her relationship with her father and possibly with Evelyn. I wonder if Mary Lou told her sister and her dad about baby Charlie's *real* dad? Did this cause issues because she came home to have her child with no promise of marriage? Maybe leaving South Bend and starting a new life in California was what she felt she had to do.

The letters didn't give too much information that I could use to find family, with the exception of one that was dated October 20, 1942.

this is on hell of a complaining letter, butch,……

one thing to lighten the burden out here for me has been the uncanny luck that I have been having at cards. Money doesn't mean much here, there is no place to spend it, so the stakes are pretty high. right now I am ahead of the game considerable more that a second lieut. makes in a year. the next time you hear from me I probably will have lost the old homestead back in tenn.

Homestead in Tennessee—could there be a Charles Edward Taylor in Tennessee? Again, the census showed hundreds of them! I tried to filter by possible birth dates of young pilots in World War II. Still, lots of Taylors. Too many! I would spend hours going through census records looking for clues.

Maybe Mary Lou and Charlie knew each other in *Indiana*. So I would plug in that state. Or there were references to Georgia, where Mary Lou had completed her military training. Was Georgia a possibility? I kept hitting roadblocks. The sheer volume of Taylors was overwhelming! When a name is plugged into the ancestry.com system, I would have the option to confirm that the data was exact, or a possibility. Since I *didn't have* an exact date, I always clicked on a *possible* date or place. Of course, this led to many more names flashing on the screen! Sorting through each possibility became more than a tad boring and disheartening.

The ancestry.com database also offered military records. Over the course of two and a half years and the nineteen letters, Charlie had risen in rank—from Captain to Major and then to

Lieutenant Colonel. I searched under all these ranks. The ancestry site also had a link to military cemeteries, and since we assumed that Charlie had died in World War II, these were carefully scoured.

Again, nothing. It was like looking for a ghost. We had the actual letters, but I couldn't find a match.

The many weeks turned into years of research. I became more and more frustrated about these roadblocks and shared my discouragement with Chuck. He was always interested but somewhat distant about my moving forward. I would always ask if he was okay with me looking for his family, and he'd always say yes. Sometimes I wondered if he might have thought it was useless for me to continue, but he never let me give up hope. The "what-ifs . . ." continued to be part of our conversation about family, even if we were both growing doubtful of finding anything about the Taylors.

My frustration led to wondering out loud with Chuck about the possibility of hiring a private detective to search for information about Chuck's dad. Maybe we could find someone who specialized in military searches. There were so many books and sources of information about World War II out there that could possibly be used. With my part-time work, we had a small financial cushion along with our retirement income, so could we use some of this to find someone to help us?

My university teaching load was growing, and I knew I'd reached the end of my research capabilities. Chuck was convinced, and we moved forward to find a professional researcher.

This was an interesting venture. Neither of us had ever hired a private detective. I almost felt as if we were living in a suspense television show. Private investigators implied secrets and drama. Maybe I had just seen too many detective shows. But we did some research, looking specifically for someone with a specialty in military persons.

A Google search helped us, and we found someone who seemed qualified. In early 2009 we made contact with a private detective and signed the paperwork. We shared the basic information of military ranks, the military identification number that was on all the letters in the return address, and the places where we knew Charlie Senior had served in World War II.

We made an initial deposit and began to wait. And wait. And wait.

Did the waiting mean that there was nothing—since the military records had possibly been burned? Or was he finding information and there was so much to tell?

Five hundred dollars later, we were given one picture of Lt. Col. Charles Edward Taylor standing by his fighter plane with several of his crew. That was it! The only fact we were able to confirm was that the picture in the shoebox, which we thought was Chuck's father, looked like the Lt. Col. Taylor in the photograph that the detective gave us. At my first look I could identify Charlie. He was standing rather casually in the middle with one hand on his hip and the other leaning against the fighter plane. Other crew members stood around him.

It seems as if the picture was a posed shot for the camera—as if they're just pals standing around and chatting, with smiles and maybe a joke. All the men are dressed in their khakis, and Charlie has his pilot's hat pushed to the back of his head with the buckle flying loose. So many fighter pilots had named their planes. But from where they were standing, no name was visible. Chuck thought the picture was probably taken for fun and did not show the seriousness of war.

There was no other identifying information on the plane or the names of the other crew members. This didn't prove or disprove that Charlie had died. All we knew was that he was a fighter pilot in World War II serving in the Asia-Pacific Theater of the war.

The detective was sure that more money would give him access to find more. Chuck and I were disappointed but not surprised. It seemed that the elusive Charlie Taylor was just not to be found. We didn't have enough confidence in the detective to continue to finance further research, so by early 2010, we were still no closer to finding Chuck's father.

Occasionally I would log on to ancestry.com and plug in Charles Edward Taylor (although I'd done that a hundred times), and hope that something would change. Can things show up differently? Would I roll the dice one day and somehow, magically, more information would appear?

I never gave up hoping; I was stubbornly committed to this even though I had no idea how to break through the impasse!

It felt like the family puzzle picture was a collage instead—independent events on a backdrop of the letters with very few connections. When I work on jigsaw puzzles, I just walk around and around the table looking for a piece to jump out at me. This wasn't happening with Chuck's family story. How many times could I circle the table? Did I have enough information about the whole story that I would even *recognize* a piece?

The Taylor family puzzle pieces were certainly not connecting into a bigger picture. The Taylor family story would be about finding the letters and a few pictures. Could I accept defeat and just leave it alone? Would these few artifacts be the sum total of the Taylor side of the family?

Only the ones living the story, Chuck and I and our daughters, would ever know how we searched. I so wanted to give Chuck and our girls more of their history! I was disappointed and had to do some self-talk about giving up.

Capt. Charles E. Taylor (center of photo, leaning against wing of plane with hand on his hip) and unidentified crew. This is the photo found by the private detective. The plane is a Curtiss P-36 Hawk. c. 1942-44.

12

New Searches for Charlie

Retirement was feeling busy. Chuck and I were carving out new interests and traveling. At this time in my life, finding more information about Chuck's father was not on my radar. I was very happy with my part-time teaching at a California state university. Additionally, I volunteered for a nonprofit board which raised monies for Meals on Wheels and a day care center for senior citizens with dementia. Life was good.

Since early 2001, one of our favorite activities was meeting our best friends, Bill and Margee, for coffee every Saturday morning. Ten o'clock sharp, and we would be ordering our lattes or espressos and sweet treats or bagels. This tradition had started at a hole-in-the-wall coffee shop located in a small strip mall with stores like Pier One, a pet store, and a Weight Watchers. There we would nod hellos to fellow locals and enjoy the quick-paced banter and fun with the owner. No matter what the weather, we seldom missed our lazy Saturday mornings.

Chuck and I usually arrived first. Our pattern was to pull several tables and chairs together on the large cemented area outside the shop to form a conversation circle. Sometimes more friends arrived, and we would just enlarge the circle. If chilly, we brought blankets and huddled closer together. If sunny and pleasant, the norm for Southern California, we sat in the shaded porch of the shop. It was a highlight of the week to relax, unwind, laugh, and connect with good friends.

Eventually the owner sold the shop, and we and a few other locals migrated to Peet's Coffee just a few blocks from the original hangout. Peet's had great coffee and sweets and worked to create a friendly atmosphere. It didn't take too long before we became comfortable as regulars.

Over the course of many Saturday mornings, our conversations meandered from politics and work stories to our children, our parents, and religion, and included lots of laughter. As our friendship grew, we began to hatch a plan to travel together. The four of us had different travel experiences but a common passion for seeing the world.

Bill and Margee had traveled to Europe many times. Their trips were often aligned with a conference for Bill who worked as a physicist. Margee had gone on many trips with him and sometimes included their children. Margee had been a piano teacher and even taught our young Jen. Then she returned to school for her doctorate in organizational psychology and taught at a community college. For years they had carved out time and were well traveled, enjoying their adventures.

I had never traveled outside of the US except to Canada and Mexico. Chuck had traveled in Europe and Southeast Asia when he served in the army. Our professions as educators gave us some larger chunks of time, but we were limited to summer travel opportunities. For years Chuck and I had dreamed of traveling to Europe, so having friends who knew the ropes made me more comfortable. As the British might say, "Let's give it a go."

We decided that if we could make this adventure happen, our first trip would be to England. An English-speaking country might be an easy first step.

We had heard from a mutual friend about hiking vacations, and this intrigued all four of us. Margee is a master at research, and she'd bring us ideas and websites to explore. We discovered a hike from village to village in the Cotswolds of England. We could hike for a week, then spend the second week in London. All through the spring of 2001, we would return to this possibility. Often over a second latte or espresso, the trip started to become more real and our excitement grew. Could we make this happen by the summer of 2002?

Unexpectedly, my father died at age ninety-three in early September 2001. On the day of his memorial service, the tragedy of 9/11 struck! Our emotions were laid bare. My father's death was sudden even though he had been in failing health. And then, the attack on our country! I felt like we were just "going through the motions" of living. Our family and colleagues were all grieving on different levels. At that time, I was a school administrator, trying to nurture my staff and our students while feeling the pain of losing my dad. The days seemed dark. Still, we were expected to be the adults, helping and supporting others while we kept our own emotions in check.

Through our pain and sadness, Saturday morning coffees continued. Our somber tone was often about the tragedy of 9/11. But this time with friends offered a calm in the storm, a comforting, warm place to share our feelings.

We all had family concerns. Bill was the main caregiver for his father, who was in his late eighties and becoming more and more frail. And what would my newly widowed mother need at age eighty-nine? She had lost her husband after sixty-four years of marriage. My siblings were involved, but Mom lived very close to us. Chuck and I would be there to support her as she adjusted and reordered her life without my dad.

As I reflect on these events, I think that just maybe, the keeper of the family history also becomes *the keeper of the family*. It was a role I gladly accepted.

The trip to England was almost put on hold. Our goal to travel together was still there, but life was happening around us and we couldn't control all of the moving parts. We were angry and concerned about our world, but as we all agreed, we were not going to stop living our lives out of fear of another surprise attack.

After many months, we were adjusting to the circumstances of a new world order with terrorists. Bill's father became more stable. My mom was adjusting amazingly well to her new life without my father. So, over a good bottle of wine, we collectively decided that our trip was back on!

In the summer of 2002, we were ready to go.

We didn't exactly know what to expect, because all our other vacations had always included hotels and cars. Nothing like hiking from village to village. We checked into the first bed-and-breakfast and were greeted by a lovely British couple who shared what we could expect from the hike. From then on, every day was filled with adventure as we walked the Cotswold Way.

Each morning before our walk began, our B-and-B hosts provided a full traditional English breakfast of coffee, eggs, sausages, sliced tomatoes, and mushrooms. Not my favorite since I don't care for eggs, but the toast and marmalade were a delicious treat. We were satisfied and eager to begin the walk.

The proprietors of the first B and B provided us with directions for the whole week's daily walks. We had no detailed map, just directions that were given to us on sheets of paper. In simple sentences, they would tell us to cross this or that field, cross over the cattle stile while watching for the bull, pass under this copper beech, continue through pastures and along trails. Every so often we would see a marking—a small circle with a triangle inside—on a fence post that indicated the Cotswold Way, so we knew we were on the correct path.

Bill took the lead, kept the directions, and forged our path. Margee and I usually walked in the middle, and Chuck brought up the rear so he could stop to take pictures and then catch up.

The very first morning of our hike was magical. After just a short distance, our hike took us to a small twelfth-century chapel. We had the place to ourselves. We just wandered around and imagined how the priests had hidden from the forces of King Henry VIII during the late fifteenth century as the Catholics were being driven from the country. What other treasures would we find as we continued to walk?

Our usual pattern was that after a half day of hiking, our directions would lead us to a small village. As the paths twisted and turned over small rises, streams, and valleys, we began to notice that we could see these villages coming—because in the distance we could see the spire on the top of a church. Our huge breakfast had become a distant memory. At the village, there would be a pub. We were always hungry and ready for the simple sandwich and a pint of the local ale. It was refreshing and gave us an opportunity to rest our weary feet. But after a short stay, we would head out for the next village. The next stop offered afternoon tea in a cozy shop. A pot of brewed tea and warm scones with clotted cream and jam, what a wonderful tradition these British folks have!

After tea, it was usually a short walking distance before we checked into our new B and B in a new village. Per our tour arrangements, we only carried small backpacks while walking, and our luggage was transported by car. Tired and ready for a short nap before dinner, we would settle in.

As the sun slowly sank on each warm summer day, we would enjoy a leisurely dinner and wine. We'd laugh and relive the day's events and marvel at our adventures. Relaxed and exhausted, and with some sore feet after eight to ten miles of walking, we were very ready for bed.

Over the course of the week of walking we didn't see any other hikers. It was surprising, but the solitude was comforting. We had the Cotswold Way to ourselves. The English countryside was a perfect place to wander, talk, build friendships, and just be with each other and nature. We couldn't have planned a more perfect holiday to cement this friendship.

Then off to London to see the Queen. (Actually, Chuck and I did see the Queen while we were at the theater to see *My Fair Lady*.)

This trip in 2002 led to another and another. Each adventure had a hiking trek followed by a city adventure. Other magical trips included the Czech Republic, France, Ireland, and then a final hiking tour in Switzerland. Each of these excursions put us in parts of the world that captured our minds with their beauty and history.

Ideas for the next destination always emerged over Saturday morning coffee hour. Before deciding on a final destination, we enjoyed shared dinners with the food and wine of the country we were hoping to visit. Margee and I both love to cook, so finding new recipes from a certain region or country gave us more appreciation of the differences in cultures. Over dinner and lots of wine, we'd discuss points of interest, search websites, review maps and travel guides, and determine our final itinerary.

All of these pre-trip events as well as the traveling excursions were carefully documented by Chuck through photos. Then on our return home, he would create an amazing video—with music! Of course, that required another dinner and more wine to watch the video and relive our trip!

Our lives changed in retirement and some difficult health issues have crept up on us all. But we continue to travel. Not hiking, but slowly sailing on river cruises—adventures at a different pace. But the planning dinners, wine sampling, and homemade videos remain a constant.

It was and still is a truly amazing friendship. Four very independent, well-educated professionals who get along famously. Our other friends marvel at our adventures. Our children seem to enjoy our traveling and encourage us. And both friends and adult children humor us by watching the videos.

It was against the backdrop of this friendship that the next piece of "finding Charlie" developed. Bill and Margee had heard the story of Chuck's family and the history of the letters. We had shared many of our thoughts and fears about what we might find as we were searching. They had supported our adventure of finding Cousin Peggy, and we told them the whole story—from moving Jen and Jeff to meeting Peggy and her husband—showing pictures of Chuck's newfound family.

By early spring of 2010, a year after our visit with Cousin Peggy, I was back into my sleuthing mode and checking ancestry.com to determine if any new databases had been added. I had learned, by trial and error, that records are constantly being added to the databases. That means that more possibilities arise for locating someone. Realizing this little trick led me to check in every so often.

One Saturday over coffee with Bill and Margee, we were chatting about our week. I eagerly shared that I had returned to researching Chuck's dad. This time I was trying to use the *rank* of Charles Edward Taylor to narrow my search. Each of Mary Lou's letters had a return address. The return address always included Charlie's rank and ID number. On the last letter, his rank was Lieutenant Colonel.

Looking back at this time, I realize that I never really stopped hoping that I would find more information. I was still assuming that Chuck's father was dead. But for some reason, on this particular Saturday, I asked the million-dollar question of Bill and Chuck. Both served in the army, so of course they would know.

"If Charlie Senior had not passed away—but had been promoted, what would his rank be?"

Without hesitation, they both said, "Colonel."

I tried to curb my excitement. Okay—a new way to filter my search. I had the possibility of a major puzzle piece; I could hardly wait to get home.

Saturday afternoon I was back at my computer, plugging in the name Col. Charles Edward Taylor. And there, there it was! *Three* Col. Taylors! All had died and were buried in military cemeteries.

I was so excited. The use of the military records had given me a new possibility! I carefully looked at each entry in the records. Up popped Col. Charles Edward Taylor who was buried in Massachusetts National Cemetery. Then another Taylor, and another.

My enthusiasm bubbled over. Our home offices were adjacent to each other, so in my excitement I called out, "Chuck, come see what I found!"

On the computer screen from the US Veterans Gravesites, ca. 1775–2006:

Name: Charles Edward Taylor

Service Info: COL US AIR FORCE WORLD WAR II, KOREA, VIETNAM

Birth Date: 18 Jul 1918

Death Date: 23 Nov 1997

Service Start: 10 Nov 1939

Date:

Interment Date: 16 Nov 1998

Cemetery: Massachusetts National Cemetery

Cemetery Address: Off Connery Avenue, Bourne, MA 02532

Buried At: Section 25 Site 540

We were both stopped in our tracks. Was this Col. Taylor Chuck's *father*? Was this the man who had written the love letters to his mother? Our beliefs and understanding about what could have happened were flipped upside down!

It was certainly a surprise and an emotional discovery. If this person was actually Chuck's father, it would mean that his father had not died in World War II . . . If the person listed on this grave marker was his father, and he had not died until 1997, why didn't Chuck have an opportunity to know him? Chuck was born in 1944. That meant *fifty-three years* of lost possibilities for a father-and-son relationship. And now, thirteen years after Col. Taylor's death, finding out that the lost years were gone forever . . .

That afternoon I continued to look at the other two Col. Taylors, just to make sure. Emotions swirled in my head. I had to admit that all the facts and timelines fit with the Col. Taylor in the Massachusetts cemetery. Was there anything else I could do to cement these facts?

I wasn't sure what steps to take next. Chuck was dealing with so many unknowns becoming knowns and new possibilities. Do I go further and continue our search? Or do I stop here?

As we processed this new information, I asked Chuck if he was okay with me diving deeper. As I've said, at each step of my research, I would ask his permission before moving further. This was *his* family, and I wanted to honor his wishes. Maybe he didn't want to know anything more. It was critical that my own curiosity not be the driver. Without even saying it, we both knew there would be pain as we moved ahead. Knowing you had a father, and that he had chosen not to be a part of your life, raises the question, what could have caused this? The letters were very much love letters, and he had talked about little Slug. He hadn't been shot down and killed. It was difficult to imagine the decision not to be a part of a son's life or his mother's.

I recall being very aware of Chuck's silences. It seemed his emotions were very raw. He is usually so calm and confident, but this was such a roller coaster of feelings! In the last year, he had found and met his cousin and discovered more about his mother's side of the family. And now this.

Over the course of the weekend, we spent time thinking about the what-ifs, and Chuck decided that he was good with moving forward. The three Col. Taylors we had discovered were just possibilities. We needed more confirmation than just the military cemetery records.

Spring of 2010 was turning out to be eventful. By Monday morning, following our Saturday discovery of the cemetery records, I was ready to place a call to the cemeteries where each Col. Taylor had been buried and see what I could learn.

Not knowing exactly what I would find, I decided to call just one cemetery first. Maybe I'd find out that I needed more information, or maybe this type of information could not be given over the phone. This first call was an experiment.

I'm not sure why I called the Massachusetts National Cemetery. But that was the first call. I had all of my information in front of me—the full name, rank, and ID number. The phone rang and rang, and then the answering machine picked up the call. I tried to succinctly put my request into words.

"My husband and I are researching family ancestry, and we were wondering if the Col. Taylor on the cemetery records is the same Taylor with the following ID number . . . ?" I left our landline phone number and then hung up.

Would this trail of research lead to the same lack of conclusions as the time we contacted James Ballou's brother? The information is shared but nothing ever comes back? Rebecca and I had both written asking for military records. We had received letters back, but they told us there had been a fire, so most of the records had been destroyed. There had been the information from the private detective with very little to show for the money. In the last thirty years we had tried several different methods with no luck. Now, I really hoped for a different outcome.

I am not a particularly patient person. I wanted results, and just having to leave the message was frustrating. But I had put this piece of the puzzle into play.

Being active is one of my coping strategies when I am waiting and trying to let things happen. In an effort to keep my mind occupied, I went out to do some errands. I had hope but no idea if we would hear from anyone at the cemetery.

After a few hours I returned home and put my packages away. I was walking up the stairs and could see directly into my office. Chuck was sitting in my office chair at my desk with his forearms resting on his legs and his head in his hands. He was calm, quiet, and slightly pale. I couldn't imagine what had happened. What news could have hit him? I quietly said, "What's going on? Are you okay?"

Then he looked up at me, and haltingly, with almost no voice, said, "This is my father."

Slowly, the details of the call came rolling out. A woman from the cemetery had heard the message and called back. At first, she told Chuck she couldn't share the information. It was confidential. But she must have wanted to give him the information because she didn't hang up immediately. In that pause, Chuck asked her again. He emphasized that he was the son and read off the ID number once more. After an extended wait, the woman said, "The number you gave me matches the soldier who is buried here."

We both just sat in my office in stunned silence.

It is hard to describe the feelings that were running through me. At first, excitement—and then the recognition that what we had just found confirmed that Chuck's father *had not died* in World War II. He had gone on to serve in Korea and Vietnam. Chuck just sat there for a long time in shock and amazement as the reality began to set in.

Unanswered questions seem to pour over us until we were swimming in them. Why had Chuck not known his father? Why did his mother keep this from him? So much emotion was churning for both of us. I couldn't imagine what Chuck was feeling. I know I was feeling anger and curiosity all mixed up.

We would need time to process this. What would we do with the information?

In the next few weeks, we'd be leaving on a river cruise from Basel, Switzerland, to Amsterdam with Bill and Margee. Once off the boat we would travel to Berlin. Chuck had been stationed in Berlin from 1965 to 1966, so he was interested in returning to see it after the wall had been torn down. The hours and conversations with Bill and Margee would be a valuable way to unwind and think through so many of the emotions of finding Col. Charles Edward Taylor. Maybe once we returned home, we would have some clarity about any next steps. Was just finding the gravestone of your father enough?

CHARLES E. TAYLOR'S MILITARY PROMOTIONS

November 10, 1939 – Joined Army Air Corps

1940 – Lieutenant

January 1942 – Captain

September 1943 – Major

February 1944 – Lieutenant Colonel

1945 – Colonel

L to R: Margee, Bill, Ann, and Chuck. Enjoying dinner after a day of hiking in the Cotswolds, England. 2002.

13

Uncovering Col. Taylor's History

$\mathcal{M}$y research skills began to move in different directions after we found the cemetery marker that gave us the life span of Col. Charles Edward Taylor. I now had some of the bigger puzzle pieces with *dates*. Still very uncertain of what else I could find, I was energized, and Chuck was supportive of the deeper dive.

Questions kept circling in my head. What had happened to break Mary Lou and Charlie apart? Did this new information about his father change how Chuck felt about his mother?

The spring of 2010 had proved to be one of discovery and shock. Having the real name and dates of birth and death gave us the opportunity—and authority—to ask for military and government records. One of the first tasks was to contact the National Archives and Records Administration to request military records. Since we could show through birth records that Chuck was Col. Taylor's legitimate son, we felt comfortable asking for the paper trail. I downloaded the request form for personnel records and completed all the required information.

Chuck signed the document, and on July 18, 2010, we mailed the request. Another waiting game was on.

However, this period of waiting didn't stop me from searching other sites. I was on a roll! One of the most interesting was a site named Critical Past. In it, when I Googled Col. Taylor, up popped a picture of him in Russia. It was on the front page of the *Waco News-Tribune* on June 25, 1956. There he was in full uniform, walking with General Twining and a Russian diplomat at the Russian Air Show! The year, 1956. Wow! Chuck is such a history buff, and he knew the background of events. At this time, the US Government was eager to build strategies to protect our country from possible Russian nuclear attack. The information that General Twining and Col. Taylor reported back to Congress was critically important. And to know that his father was involved!

The heading under the picture reads:

AFTER THE SHOW - General Nathan F. Twining (left), Chief of Staff of the U.S. Air Force, is shown leaving Tushino Airfield in Moscow Sunday after observing a huge air show there in commemoration of Soviet Air Force Day. He is accompanied by Col. Charles Taylor (center), U.S. air attaché in Moscow, and an unidentified Soviet Air Force liaison officer. (UP Radiotelephoto)

How did Charlie get from Hawaii with Mary Lou to Russia? What had happened between his last letter to Mary Lou in October 1944, and his appearing on the front page of the *Waco News-Tribune* in 1956 with a general in Russia?

I continued to explore this site and found out that we could order an enlarged reproduction of the front page of the newspaper. I placed the order along with $20. The picture was on its way. Chuck and I were both just amazed by this pictorial treasure. The idea that his father had been in Moscow as an air attaché was a bit mind blowing.

What was Col. Taylor doing in Russia? Did he have a family and were they with him? The picture came a few weeks later. Even though the quality is very grainy, it continued to intrigue us.

This picture added new dimensions to who Col. Taylor was. For years Chuck had the image of his natural father as a fighter pilot. But this picture indicated that he held an important military position. This only intensified our desire to know more.

About the same time as finding the *Waco News-Tribune* picture, I found a site that had short film clips of historical newsreels. The clips were organized by events and dates. Painstakingly, I searched clip after clip looking for film around the early 1950s and the Russian Air Show in Moscow.

As I was searching, the task became so tedious! I found myself drifting out of focus and remembering my own personal memories during the 1950s.

I was a young teenager in the late '50s, and my best friend was Susie. One of our favorite things to do was to go to the movies on a Saturday afternoon. I'm sure we felt so grown up just walking down one of the main streets lined with stores and shops. Just the two of us. We were usually seeing the latest Pat Boone or Doris Day movie, but before the main feature there would be newsreels.

As I was growing up, my family received newspapers—morning and evening—thrown on our wide front porch. I can remember the thump of the paper hitting the porch long before I was fully awake. My dad had trained our cocker spaniel, Mac, to fetch the paper. Every morning, bright and early, my dad and Mac would head to the kitchen for morning coffee and to read the newspaper. Then in the afternoon, another paper would arrive

The Ribbon Untied

around four o'clock that would feature news of the day, often showcasing lots of local events. Television news was not a part of our family viewing, so between the radio and the newspapers, we learned what was happening around the world and in our city.

But at the movies, we would be able to see *live action*. As I looked through these clips searching for Col. Taylor, I was able to put myself back into the big chairs of the dark movie theater with Susie at my side as world news flashed across the screen! I can still hear the dramatic music and the deep voice of the narrator describing the action before us. The world seemed like a dangerous place with the Korean War conflict and the threat of bombs being dropped by Russia. Of course, the two of us didn't pay too much attention. We were young girls, looking at the romance of the movies and heading out to have a hot-fudge sundae at the drugstore afterwards.

I kept recalling my past as I typed "Col. Taylor" into the database of newsclips. And suddenly, *there was Col. Taylor* walking across the computer screen! I found a live-action clip! I couldn't believe it. It was the same image we had seen on the front page of the *Waco News-Tribune* from the air show in Moscow. There was Col. Taylor, air attaché to Moscow, US General Twining, and the Russian officer walking together toward the camera.

I think in that moment I felt a stab of pain, realizing that a father and son would never really know each other. Father and son would never laugh together, play football on the front lawn, make pancakes on Sunday mornings. Son would never be yelled at to "turn the music down." No chance to just pal around.

I was trying to keep this piece of new information away from Chuck because I was beginning to hatch a plan to surprise him with all the pieces I had found. But my excitement eclipsed everything else. I yelled over to Chuck in his office, "Come see what I found!"

Seeing the *walk* of Col. Taylor created such validation for me. I had known Chuck since I was sixteen, and Col. Taylor's walk was my husband's walk! And now, almost fifty years later, through this short clip, I was meeting my husband's *father*. I knew that walk, that tall stance, the way his shoulders swayed as he walked! Their movements were so much alike!

Tears filled my eyes. This was truly Chuck's father.

I have read all the letters from Charlie to Mary Lou hundreds of times. Almost every time I read them I cry, as I can see so much of my Chuck in his father's letters. Chuck and I had written letters to each other for over four years, and I have kept them all. Those hundreds of letters give me written records of his feelings, his humor, his personal being. His father's letters contained so many of the same feelings, his humor, and his personality. I knew in my gut that Chuck and Charlie were son and father from the first time we found the letters in the shoebox. This clip showing the Taylor walk just confirmed my gut reaction to be true.

The newspaper picture and the film kept adding pieces to who Col. Taylor was. Chuck is a student of history, and he knew so much about this period of the Cold War during the 1950s and early '60s. Chuck had also been stationed in West Berlin in 1964 during the Cold War and had firsthand experience with the political anxiety of armed forces in the four-power city of West Berlin. How had his father interfaced with the Russians? What was his role as air attaché? Chuck knew immediately that air attaché meant spy and espionage. Chuck keeps so much of his emotion under check, but I felt like he was processing all of these discoveries and trying to put his father in a context. The historical

148

significance of the Russian Air Show is talked about in the history books. The results that General Twining and Col. Taylor reported to Congress were key factors in creating the Strategic Air Command (SAC). But in terms of Chuck's history, the significance of finding Col. Taylor was just coming into focus. How would knowing all of these interesting historical events change his feelings about who his father was?

Discoveries about Col. Taylor continued through the summer of 2010. On August 2, the National Personnel Records Center responded, and once again we were blown away with new information. The military records we received were the Separation documents, fondly referred to as DD 214s. When a soldier leaves the military service, this document is completed. It's basically a one-page summary of a soldier's career. The letters to Mary Lou tell one side of Charlie Taylor through his love, humor, and emotions. But these DD 214 documents cemented the details of Col. Taylor's career in the military. We were beginning to see a fuller picture of his life, even in tiny slivers.

Because Chuck had been in the military and had received his own DD 214, he read this and quickly understood the gold mine we had just received. There were two DD 214s. Chuck scanned the first and discovered that his father had retired January 31, 1970. The second DD 214 showed that Charlie spent another year on reserve before leaving active duty.

In these pages we were able to see Col. Taylor's place of birth—Welch, West Virginia. His education from war colleges to Russian language school. His blood type, A negative. His military specialty, Intelligence Staff Officer. And all of his decorations, medals, badges, commendations, citations, and campaign ribbons—so many that it filled the space with abbreviations!

It also stated permanent addresses for mailing purposes after retirement.

The surprises just kept coming. Another Google search yielded another newspaper, the *Frederick Post* in Frederick, Virginia, dated October 4, 1954. Again, on the front page, was a very small article with the headline:

UNDERGOES SURGERY

Moscow, Oct. 3 AP   US Air Force Col. Charles Taylor new air attaché here, was stricken with appendicitis when he arrived here Friday and was operated on at the Moscow Polyclinic Hospital. He is reported to be in "good condition" today.

Mrs. Taylor said her husband was receiving good treatment and had no complaints to make. He was believed to be the first American official to undergo an operation in a Soviet hospital.

Here was new information: a *Mrs.* Taylor. She must have been with him in Moscow. Were there any children? Could Chuck have half brothers or sisters? Did his mother ever know about where Col. Taylor was? By the time of these events in Russia, Mary Lou had married Gustav Eklund, lived in California, and worked as a nurse in a veterans hospital. Chuck had been adopted and his name was changed to Charles Edward Eklund. Chuck would have been in elementary school. Both he and his mother would have been suffering the violent abuse of his stepfather.

I find that as I write about all these discoveries, I still have anger about the way things turned out. I am not sure if it's anger at Mary Lou, or Chuck's real father, or his stepfather. It just seems to ooze out every so often.

Other official documents were also available. I quickly made use of the data and ordered a death certificate. Again, more information.

DEATH: Bedford, Massachusetts.

NAME OF SPOUSE: Carol Swiss.

PARENTS NAMES AND BIRTH PLACES: John Edward Taylor born in Tennessee. Vina Phillips born in Tennessee. Residence at time of death: Somerville, Massachusetts.

CAUSE OF DEATH: Aspiration Pneumonia Urinary Tract Infection Alzheimer's Dementia.

All of this information added to the bigger picture. (So the old homestead in Tennessee that Charlie almost lost in the poker game was real.) Maybe even some of the most difficult puzzle pieces were starting to fit together.

Chuck now had names and places where his father and grandparents had lived. Charlie had been born in Welch, West Virginia. Was Chuck's grandfather a coal miner? With this information I was able to return to the census records on ancestry.com and locate the towns where they lived. Through these records I discovered that Grandmother Vina had a twin sister, China. Chuck and I had a good laugh about that. He wasn't too sure about his ancestors being southerners. He hoped they had not been slave owners.

We now had a name for Charlie's wife: Carol. This would have been the woman who was quoted in the newspaper about Col. Taylor's appendicitis in Moscow. Was she still living? And if so, where? Was she still at the residence in Somerville, Massachusetts?

It was interesting for both of us to know how his father had died. Our oldest daughter, Jennifer, has a doctorate in genome science, so we have had many discussions about genetic links and possible health issues. We wondered about the Alzheimer's dementia link. Seeing that Chuck's father was seventy-nine when he died, and Chuck had just turned sixty-seven, should we be concerned?

It's hard to imagine that one piece of paper can bring so many things into your emotional being! We had facts. We had places. We had names. All of these connected in some fashion. But sometimes I was just stopped in my tracks.

All of our research activities and family history discoveries from 2010 had melted into the spring of 2011. Patience is not one of my virtues, and this hunting for family takes lots of time. It demands perseverance and a willingness to let go when a link doesn't seem to pan out. Fortunately, I was enjoying my teaching at the university and keeping very busy. The waiting for documents was just part of the process of continuing our search.

For months I had this thought in the back of my mind. What if I could surprise Chuck with a trip to the cemetery where his father was buried? Father's Day in mid-June and Chuck's birthday, June 24, seemed like an appropriate time to give him this gift of finding his father. The DD 214s and the death certificate gave me so many geographical points to connect for a trip.

Our good friend Debbie was a travel agent. I decided to ask her to help me plan. I think Debbie was as excited as I was to help me make this happen. Chuck and I both loved Boston, so our trip could start there. The itinerary would need to include going to the cemetery on Cape Cod, and traveling to Somerville to see where Charlie had been living when he died. There, we would also research in the Somerville library to look for an obituary. Chuck and I had been to Boston a few years previously, and Debbie had arranged that trip, so we were in good hands.

Debbie planned an amazing journey. She booked us into the Dan'l Webster Inn on Cape Cod, an old inn that was steeped in American history. From here we could make our daily trips into Somerville, a neighborhood in the greater Boston area. We also had easy access to the cemetery. It looked quite good.

I would give Chuck the gifts of the tickets and trip plans, accompanied by a binder that compiled all the details we knew about Charles Edward Taylor, Sr.!

Over the next few weeks in early May 2011, I found and printed out information on Charlie's hometown, Welch, West Virginia, and included a map of the area. I printed out census records that showed Chuck's grandparents in Tennessee—John Taylor and Vina Phillips. I carefully researched each of the medals that Col. Taylor had received as noted on the DD 214s. I found pictures of each of these medals and their specific meanings. I made a page for each medal. The book included the picture from the air show in Russia from the *Waco News-Tribune*. The small article about the appendicitis attack would also have a page.

While I was busy planning this surprise, another very interesting bit of information was discovered. Just Googling Col. Taylor's name, I discovered that he had been shot down in Tokyo Bay in 1945 and recovered by a US submarine, the *Razorback*. In Wikipedia, buried deep in the history of the submarine, was an account of this incident.

On 7 May "Razorback" headed west again. Assigned to lifeguard duty in the Nanpo Island and Tokyo Bay areas, she rescued Lieutenant Colonel Charles E. Taylor, a P-51 fighter pilot from the 21st Fighter Group on 25 May. On 5 June she rescued four B-29 Superfortress crewmen shot down during an air raid over Kobe, Japan . . .

I shared this find with Chuck. We both wondered if his mother had known about this. The incident would have happened after Chuck was born in June 1944, and after the letters had stopped in October 1944. Chuck remembers that incident in the bathroom when his mother had said, "Your real father was a pilot, and shot down in World War II in the Pacific."

Could this incident with the *Razorback* be what she was referencing?

We'll never know. But the *Razorback* story would certainly have a page in the surprise gift book.

Father's Day weather was beautiful and sunny. Our large paver-stone patio was the scene where we'd hosted many parties. On this day we would celebrate Father's Day and Chuck's birthday outside in this special place. Chuck had designed the patio with many of his personal touches—roses and birch trees. Running the full length of the yard were birch trees, gently rustling. On both sides of the patio are rose beds, and the June rose bloom was magnificent!

Of course, Bill and Margee were part of the celebration. Our Rebecca was also home. Her culinary talents had helped with the preparation. I always ask Chuck what he wants for his special dinner, and the answer is always the same. We enjoyed our big juicy hamburgers—cooked to perfection by Chuck—with slices of purple onion and American cheese, along with Rebecca's special potato salad. Then boysenberry pie à la mode!

Finally, I handed Chuck the notebook—just a blue three-ring binder with "Charles Edward Taylor, Sr." in big letters on the slip-in title page. On the front of the binder I had added a few stickers that were red, white, and blue. Very simple. The love and care were inside!

Once Chuck realized what he had, I don't think he could talk. He just sat there. I was thrilled to have pulled it off—knowing I have a hard time keeping secrets! Bill and Margee and Rebecca had been in the know, so it was fun for them to see Chuck so surprised.

As I think about the events leading up to that day, I am still in awe of the person Chuck is. He didn't know his real father, but so much of what we have discovered about Charlie has definitely been passed on to Chuck. His mother was not one to nurture or praise her son, but she took care of him. Whether it's nature or nurture, Chuck became this incredible person.

After all the excitement about the pending trip, Chuck and I were able to sit back and look at what we knew now about his father. In just the last few months, a new picture was emerging. From the fighter pilot to a colonel who had been involved in some of the most intriguing, interesting, and tense times of American history! It was hard to imagine Col. Taylor's life as an intelligence officer. Since Chuck had been in Germany, he had some feel for the sensitive and fragile nature of the European peace. He has always been fascinated by the systems at work and the leadership decisions. We were mind blown to think that Chuck's father was a part of that period in history.

The trip to the Boston area was on our agenda for the fall of 2011. It was going to be exciting to plan the bits and pieces and figure out how we could use every moment.

But before the Boston trip, we left for another summer trip with Bill and Margee. This time we headed to Basel, Switzerland. We boarded a riverboat and cruised down the Rhine toward Amsterdam, Holland. We'd spend a week on the riverboat, then we would disembark and go by train to Berlin.

Chuck was very excited about the upcoming visit to Berlin. When he was stationed there in 1964–65, the Berlin Wall was standing. Over the years in his storytelling, he'd share episodes of skirmishes between US soldiers and the East Germans or the Russians. To see the wall in ruins would be an emotional event for him.

But as we floated down the Rhine, Chuck would sometimes stay on board while Bill and Margee and I went ashore for the daily excursions. Chuck complained about being very tired. Little did we know where this was leading.

John Edward Taylor (Grandpa Eddie) and wife, Vina Phillips Taylor (Grandma Vina), parents of Charles Edward Taylor. Kentucky, c. 1940s.

AFTER THE SHOW—General Nathan F. Twining (left), Chief of Staff of the U. S. Air Force, is shown leaving Tushino Airfield in Moscow on Sunday after observing a huge air show there in commemoration of Soviet Air Force Day. He is accompanied by Col. Charles Taylor (center), U. S. air attache in Moscow, and an unidentified Soviet Air Force liaison officer. (UP Radiotelephoto)

Newspaper clipping from the *Waco News-Tribune* describing the events at the Soviet Air Show in 1956.

The Ribbon Untied

14

Chuck's Heart Surgery

By mid-August we were home again. I was settling in for another semester of teaching, and Chuck was back into retirement mode, enjoying his photography and creating the video from our recent river cruise.

A few days into our return on a very hot summer morning, Chuck woke me up to ask, "Has Rebecca maybe left one of her inhalers for her asthma downstairs?"

In my morning drowsiness I asked, "Why? What's going on?"

He shared that he hadn't been sleeping too well for a few nights. Then this last evening he was looking on the internet trying to diagnose himself. It must be "late onset of asthma." He was convinced he just needed that inhaler.

I immediately said, "We are going to the emergency room. This is not asthma."

We lived five minutes from our local hospital, so no 911 calls for us. I could get there much faster. Chuck was taken immediately into the emergency room, past all the other persons waiting.

Emergency rooms were no secret to me. Our daughter Rebecca had—and still has—frequent health issues. I have sat through hospital waits too numerous to recall. But this one was different. My Chuck was here, and we didn't know what was wrong. And the quickness of the emergency room staff made me anxious.

Once he was in the bed and hooked up to all the necessary equipment, I was allowed to join him. He had shared his asthma diagnosis with the doctor. Tests were run and we waited.

After what seemed like forever, the emergency room doctor came back in and sat down next to Chuck by the side of the bed and said, "Now tell me again, why do you think you have adult late onset of asthma?"

Chuck responded, "Well, I have shortness of breath, and I haven't been sleeping very well for several nights. It feels like my heart is flipping over."

The doctor spoke very definitively with little to no emotion. "You do not have asthma. You have congestive heart failure. We will be calling in a cardiologist."

Then the physician got up and left the room. Chuck went pale and seemed in total shock. The nurse had been standing at the door listening. She immediately came to Chuck and said, "You've never heard that before, have you?"

Chuck shook his head. "No."

Then she said, "That does *not* mean that you're going to die." She explained that the cardiologist would come and talk with him about treatment and next steps.

I just stood there, also in shock. I heard the scary words. I knew Chuck had a heart murmur. He was under a cardiologist's care and took medicine for this condition. But this seemed way too serious.

I crossed the room and grabbed Chuck's hand. We just looked at each other. It was quiet except for all the beeping noises from the machines. Slowly, I think I began to talk about his cardiologist. Chuck had great faith in Dr. Hess, so we would wait to hear from him. We both knew it was serious. But we had no clue about what the future would hold. What was wrong with Chuck's heart?

The next steps were difficult. Dr. Hess was not in town and would be back from his vacation in three days. This meant that another hospital-assigned cardiologist and hospitalist would be coming to give their assessment about treatment. We tried to reassure ourselves and remain confident. This hospital has an excellent reputation for cardiac care and open-heart surgery.

It is interesting to look back and think about how one handles these emotional stressors. I didn't want to dwell on the what-ifs of "heart failure." My pattern is to immediately go into organizational behavior: Who needed to know? What about the cats at home? What about my teaching? I often get ahead of myself and start imagining the worst-case scenario.

What I did know was that I needed the support of family and Bill and Margee. I first called Jen and Jeff in Seattle and then Rebecca, who was living with us off and on. Jen wanted to come immediately but knew we needed to wait until we knew more. Rebecca was already on her way to the hospital.

I'm sure many daughters have special bonds with their dads. I had certainly witnessed this with Jen and Rebecca. Chuck could get them to laugh. He could tease them without putting them down. Sunday mornings he always won the pillow fighting contest through roars of laughter. He read bedtime stories and played games. He helped with homework and science fair projects. He had them help him as he built them a large playhouse. He participated in family meetings. When we traveled, he gave mini history and geography lessons. He showed them wonders in nature. With his gift as a photographer, he could capture them in moments of happiness, joy, contemplation, or concern. He taught them to drive—patient and calm! He defended them when boyfriends were not kind. He moved them into new apartments and traveled across the country with their cats. He was there for them. He showed them a father's love and how to love.

I knew that for the girls, having their dad in the hospital with a potential life-threatening problem would be difficult. I needed to be there for them as they were for me.

Then I called Bill and Margee. I knew I could turn to them for support and comfort. They were at the hospital in minutes. I left Chuck for a few minutes to meet them in the emergency waiting room. I gave them an abbreviated version of what was going on. They offered to do anything and reassured me they were there for us. After a big hug they were off to wait for information about the next steps. Good friends are priceless!

The next few days seemed like a blur. There were tests and doctors giving Chuck assessments of what needed to be done. He had a heart valve problem and was in severe A-fib (Atrial fibrillation). The recommendation was for open-heart surgery to replace the mitral valve. Chuck would listen to the doctors and ask a few questions. If a valve replacement, would it be an artificial valve, or a pig or cow valve? I recall that the hospitalist, who is not a cardiologist, seemed to be putting pressure on Chuck to move ahead with the valve replacement surgery—but with no other options being given. By now Chuck was stable and knew that his doctor would be home from his vacation soon. Chuck wanted Dr. Hess's assessment. He pushed back calmly and firmly. "I'll wait for Dr. Hess."

Four days after Chuck had been admitted, Dr. Hess was on the scene. The scenario quickly changed. I did not know Dr. Hess except to say hello, but I could see that Chuck was calmer. Dr. Hess knew Chuck and wanted to give him some additional tests which he administered himself. I felt Chuck was in good hands.

The test results indicated that Chuck's heart and all the veins and arteries leading in and out of his heart were in good condition. That was all really good news. The problem was the valve— just not opening and closing correctly and letting blood rush back into the heart.

Dr. Hess offered another alternative: a heart valve *repair*. "This repair procedure is very new, and there are only a few surgeons who are now implementing this treatment. Dr. Starnes developed this technique for valve repair, and he's affiliated with the University of Southern California. I heard him speak about this procedure at a recent medical conference. If you agree, I'll contact Dr. Starnes to see if he will take your case."

Yes, Dr. Starnes would take the case! But Chuck needed to be at the Keck Hospital of USC *that same evening* in order to have surgery the next morning!

I don't know when I've seen such fast and efficient action in a hospital. Usually, it's "hurry up and wait." But now calls were being made, and nurses and attendants were busy getting Chuck ready to be discharged. Within a few hours, a cardiac nurse and her team were there with an ambulance to transport Chuck to the Keck Hospital of USC in downtown Los Angeles.

Chuck now recalls that it was the most uncomfortable ride of his life—lying there on that stretcher, bouncing on the US 101 freeway through rush-hour traffic! Of course, he always sees the humor as he recounts this wild ride.

The cardiac nurse had brought an intern into the ambulance with her. She was training the intern, and as they watched Chuck's heart monitor and vital signs, she would tell her student exactly what was going on. Of course, Chuck was hearing it all. As they traveled along the freeway—no sirens—there were several hospitals along the way. And at each freeway off-ramp close to a hospital, the ambulance driver would call back, "Is the patient okay? Or do I need to divert to the closest hospital?" Fortunately, no off-ramp diversions!

The trip continued and about an hour and a half later Chuck arrived at USC. Within minutes he was being pushed up to his new room where he would stay the night and be readied for surgery the next morning.

I'm glad I didn't know all the details about Chuck's ambulance trip until it was over. I get Chuck's humor now, but at the time it wouldn't have seemed too funny. I was just relieved that Chuck was going to be under the care of one of the top cardiac surgeons in the greater Los Angeles area. All good! The Keck Hospital is a teaching hospital, and this was also a relief.

Rebecca had been a great source of strength and support during Chuck's stay at the local hospital. She had recently completed her certification at the Santa Barbara College of Culinary Arts and was working at Panera Bread in the food-service industry. Between her work hours she visited her dad. Now, this afternoon, she was acting as my freeway guide and navigator.

Traversing the LA freeway system is a bit tricky, and I didn't mind doing the freeway driving. But my brain was in somewhat of a fog. The five days at the local hospital had been stressful, and watching Chuck face surgery added to that. I generally handle stress well, but having Rebecca there to navigate the

The Ribbon Untied

freeway system was very comforting. I could just concentrate on the driving.

We thought we would follow the ambulance, but in rush-hour traffic it was not possible and probably not a wise plan. Rebecca was able to read off the signs and guide me into the correct lane to exit. This was really helpful because I would be making this ninety-minute trip by myself over the next many days. Just hearing her say, out loud, the names of the routes and the exits cemented the directions in my memory.

She and I arrived late in the afternoon with the hot August sun beating down on us. We found our way into the parking lot maze next to the busy, loud city hospital. The Keck Hospital of USC is a large campus of multistoried buildings. People were streaming in and out. Doctors and nurses and hospital staff in scrubs all over the place. Family and friends of hospital patients wandering like we were. It was like a *beehive* with people coming and going, noisy and hot. At the parking kiosk we received a map and our directions. Quickly we found the correct building and entrance. Inside, we felt the cool of the air-conditioned building, smelled the antiseptic smell, and were greeted by a quiet calm.

It took a few moments to get our bearings. A few long halls and several elevators later, we arrived in Chuck's room. Chuck was sitting up in bed, seemingly calm. He has an amazing ability to see humor in so many difficult situations. There he was, making Rebecca and me laugh. He shared about the wild, uncomfortable ride in the ambulance and the cardiac nurse training the intern.

Then he went on to regale us with the story of the young candy stripers. Just minutes before we arrived, two candy stripers had come in to check his bottom to look for bedsores. He thought it was so funny. I'm sure he made them laugh as he joked about an old man's butt. He told us about the special bath to get all the potential germs off of his entire body. He called it the "heebie-jeebie" treatment that he would have to do that night before surgery the next morning.

All in all, he was in good spirits. We also joked about being at USC. As a teenager and throughout his adult life, he had been a fan of USC football and all the traditions of Trojan sports. Being at USC wasn't the worst place to be. We probably all hummed a few bars of the fight song and then laughed together. That helped ease our stress.

Rebecca and I sat and visited while some of the rush-hour travel subsided before we headed home. She and I gave Chuck our good-byes and love yous. Leaving was hard for me. I didn't want Chuck to be alone. But I knew he was in the best place, and that tomorrow would be a new day.

Over the last few days, the girls and I had been communicating often. Both of them wanted to be there for their dad and me. Rebecca had recently started a new job, so missing work didn't seem wise. Jen had wanted to come. But after much discussion, we decided it would be better to wait until her dad was home and recovering.

I was trying to be strong and handle this myself. I knew the day of surgery would be long. At home, I packed some magazines and my iPad and readied myself for bed.

Lying in bed without Chuck was very sobering. And lonely.

I prayed and had faith that he would have a successful surgery, but I felt so lost just lying with the empty space next to me. The last time we were in bed together had been six nights before. I wondered how many more before he would be home.

I found myself imagining life without him, and the sense of loss was overwhelming. I moved my hand over to the space where he would be sleeping, cuddled up with one of our cats, and tried to fall asleep.

I'm sure I did not sleep well, thinking about what lay ahead and the anticipation of an early rise. I wanted to get a head start on the long drive to the hospital. It was important to me to be able to see Chuck *before* the surgery. I made it just in time!

Chuck appeared calm, but I could feel his anxiety underneath his smile and hello. Shortly after I arrived, he was given a sedative even before being wheeled down the hall. The staff arrived with the gurney ready to take Chuck for surgery. As if sensing my fear, the transport staff person smiled and invited me to walk along Chuck's side as they went to the elevator. After a strong hand squeeze and quick kiss, I could see that Chuck was fading into sleep. By the time we arrived at the elevator, he was out and under the sedative. Off he went.

I just stood at the elevator door and watched it close. The next time I would see Chuck would be in his room in the cardiac intensive care unit (cardiac ICU).

I was given instructions about where to wait, and I was told that the doctor would come to see me in six or seven hours, after the surgery. Many elevators and long halls later, I found the waiting room lobby. I began to settle in for the long wait.

But within a few minutes of arranging my purse and books, I looked up to see two dear friends, Margee and Suzanne! They didn't tell me they were coming—just arrived. Suzanne had lost her husband to cancer a few years before, so she knew the fear and anxiety of waiting. She and Margee had driven down to be with me. I really received their love as we all embraced in a big hug.

And then we sat, huddled together in the waiting room, trying to pass the time with small talk and chatter, trying *not* to discuss the fear and anxiety that shadowed over us. During the hours of waiting, we went for coffee and lunch. We walked the gardens of the hospital. Concerned that I would miss the doctor, I was always careful to tell the attendant at the desk where I was going.

Late in the afternoon, Dr. Starnes walked in. Margee and Suzanne stayed beside me as we listened to the results of the surgery. Dr. Hess had been correct. Chuck was a good candidate for the valve repair, even though this was a dangerous surgery. The doctor explained how he was able to go through Chuck's side, spread the ribs apart, put the heart on a machine to keep it working, and do the repair! The medical profession calls this less invasive than the traditional open-heart surgery. Didn't seem *less invasive* to me! But in this procedure, it is not necessary to crack open the chest cavity, just to bend some ribs to get to the heart.

Dr. Starnes reassured us in a calm, quiet voice, saying, "It has all gone smoothly, and Chuck is in recovery now." He said Chuck would be in the hospital for a few days, and as he regained his strength he would be "good as new!" I would be able to see him in a few hours.

Our sighs of relief were audible. "Thank you, Baby Jesus!" This phrase had become somewhat of a joke from another mutual friend, but it wasn't a joke in this instance, and it certainly seemed to fit here. I was feeling numb. It was such a comfort to have Margee and Suzanne with me, but they needed to head home in the rush-hour traffic. I am usually the hostess who is making sure everyone else is okay, but now my role was reversed.

The Ribbon Untied

These dear friends were making sure I was okay. I would be just fine. A few long hugs and they were on their way.

I quickly called Jen and Rebecca to tell them that their dad was out of surgery and that everything had gone well. Hearing their voices was so comforting, and sharing the good news was a cause to celebrate.

During the next several hours of waiting to see Chuck, I just sat there. I had talked with our girls and my friends were gone. Nothing to do but wait and count my blessings. There were many things to comfort me—high-quality health care, loving family and friends, and my loving husband was on his way to recovery.

All hospitals seem to have these somewhat sterile waiting rooms that they try to make comfortable. For me, the waiting area seemed a bit surreal. The seats were placed in small group-ings around the room, and there were a few plants. The chairs were scratchy upholstery or fake leather. The indoor/outdoor carpet offered some attempt at softness. I could hear the buzz of the air-conditioning and an occasional telephone ring, but mostly, it was quiet.

By now the room had emptied. Chuck's surgery had been long, and all the other waiting family and friend groups had left. My magazines and computer games held no interest. My mind was blank, and I had an overwhelming sense of exhaustion, both physically and mentally.

It seemed like forever before I was called to make my way back through the long halls and multiple elevators to find the car-diac ICU. When I entered, I was greeted by a nurse. He told me that Chuck was doing fine, then immediately asked me, "Have you ever seen someone coming out of this type of surgery?"

"No," I responded.

He explained that Chuck was hooked up to many machines, tubes, and bags of fluid. The nurse didn't want me to be surprised or worried. This was *normal.*

Then he led me in, and true to his word, there were multiple poles with fluids dripping, machines beeping, and tubes going into Chuck everywhere. He was quietly lying there with his eyes closed, surrounded by equipment. I slowly approached, and in a hushed voice I called his name. He opened his eyes and gave me a small smile. It was so good to see him, but all that equipment!

The nurse shared what was going on. Throughout Chuck's recovery over the next few days, someone would be in the room with him—or very close by—24/7. "As his body starts to heal and return to normal functioning, all of this equipment will gradually be removed."

I could only see Chuck for a few minutes before I was asked to leave. Again, we shared a hand squeeze, a short kiss, and I promised to see him in the morning.

The procedures and protocols were impressive. It seemed that his care would be excellent, and slowly he would heal and be up and about. Chuck and I both like to be in control, but experiences like this made me realize that some situations are way beyond our control. Letting go and trusting others takes a leap of faith. I had to be okay with having others in charge.

The days of recovery in the hospital had ups and downs. On the first day, he was sitting on the side of the bed. He walked a few steps the next day. Meanwhile, he chatted with his nurse, found humor, and entertained the hospital staff.

Bill, Margee, and their son Rick, a young doctor, were his first visitors. Then other friends came. I usually arrived bright and early and stayed until late afternoon or into the evening. After about four days, Chuck was told he would be going home. Yay!

I arrived next morning fully expecting to be driving him home in a few hours. But it wasn't to be. The A-fib had returned! Home plans were canceled. We were both so disappointed, and once again a fear factor set in. What was wrong now?

As I drove home that evening without bringing Chuck, the loneliness flooded my whole being. Would the doctors be able to get the A-fib under control? What were the long-lasting effects of this type of condition? Had the valve repair truly been success-ful? Chuck and I had built our lives together, and I couldn't fathom being without him. I know others have lost those they love, but I wasn't ready. I just kept telling myself: one day at a time. This trip home also brought up the loss of my dad and my mother. And only two years before, I had lost my brother to cancer. Too many losses.

The next day, a new treatment plan was put in place to get Chuck's heart rhythms under control. Some very strong medicine and a treatment to reset the heart. Everything seemed to be work-ing, and slowly Chuck was getting better.

Being at a teaching hospital has its pros and cons. On the pro side, there are some very bright young doctors working with experienced physicians who are usually very well known and respected in their specialty. This was certainly the case at Keck Hospital. Having a team approach usually creates good solutions. Dr. Starnes's team was exceptional and very responsive. They had a plan for Chuck, and it seemed to be working.

On the con side, a team means a lot of individuals involved in your care. And these young residents wanted to impress Dr. Starnes. Chuck had lots of visits from young docs who often asked the same questions over and over. And then when Dr. Starnes did his rounds with the team, the room would be filled with all the team members. Also, many different residents wanted to weigh in on the proper course of treatment, so there were a variety of medicines given.

Several days later I was there at the hospital, ready to bring him home. We learned that after you have heart surgery, you are not allowed to sit in the front seat because of possible airbag injury. Chuck was safely buckled into the back seat with a pillow over his chest to ease the pressure of the seat belt. Fortunately, the ride home was a bit more gentle than Chuck's ambulance ride seven days prior!

Home never felt so good! After twelve long days in two hospitals, my love was home and on his way to recovery.

Once he was settled in the big lounge chair in our bedroom, Madison the cat gave him an inspection. She did it as only a cat can do, sniff, sniff, sniff up and down his chest, around his face and head. Then she settled down, curling up in Chuck's lap for a nap. All was well.

I think I would agree with the cat. All seemed well.

After a few days at home there was one worrisome episode that required a trip to the local hospital emergency room by ambulance. But the cause seemed to be medication, which Dr. Hess quickly identified and adjusted.

Finally, it seemed Chuck was ready to return to a more normal routine as a happy retired guy. It had been quite the ordeal, and Chuck and I were both ready to put it behind us. Our trip to Boston and Cape Cod had been put on hold for the heart problems. Now we were eager to think about the possibility of traveling the following spring, 2012.

Health issues in families bring up lots of questions. And when you don't know your whole family history, much can be left to the imagination. Finding the death certificate for Chuck's father was interesting, but it did not tell us anything about heart problems. Chuck remembered that his mother had some issues with her heart, but he couldn't recall the details. She had died of lung cancer which had traveled to her brain. The probable cause was her heavy smoking from a very early age. If we could find more information about Col. Taylor, there may be some health clues that could be helpful—maybe or maybe not. We just surmised about the possibilities.

Life did not settle in as routinely as we had expected. Just a few weeks after Chuck was home, Rebecca fell, which resulted in torn tissue in her right ankle. The diagnosis was that she needed surgery to repair it. This would have been her seventh ankle surgery.

Surgeries were part of our life with Rebecca. We had sat through many, in so many hospital waiting rooms. Would this be just another bump in the road for her? Here she was with her new culinary training, ready to begin her career. And now another ankle surgery.

We assumed the surgery would be routine and that she would be up and back at work in a few weeks. Unfortunately, Rebecca's wound did not heal, so she required yet another surgery.

Chuck was great at helping with wound care. He is very attentive and organizes the process of removing the old bandage and preparing the new one. Once Rebecca was home, the bandage had to be cleaned and rewrapped every day. This was the routine. We all anticipated the stitches coming out soon. She and her dad could compare wounds and laugh about hospitals!

I was tired of hospital parking lots, hospital food, hospital smells, and so tired of the waiting! Again, a lot of self-talk: *Stay calm . . . one foot in front of the other.* We would get through this and be laughing on the other side.

As 2011 began to wind down, Jen and Jeff came for a visit over the Christmas holidays. They always bring joy, fun, and lots of laughter. Jeff's little daughter, Becca, came with them along with Jeff's mom. It was a full house.

To add to the excitement, we bought a dog on December 29, 2011. In Chuck's recovery from heart surgery, it was important for him to stay active. And a dog would be the perfect medicine!

A beautiful Siberian husky stole our hearts as she looked at us from the pet-store window. Throughout the year we had been researching different dog breeds. It had been years since our big malamute, Oreo, had died, and we now had a large variety of cats which we loved. But we needed more regular exercise, so a new dog was a good excuse.

Chuck prevailed in the family naming contest. He named her Gabrielle after Gabrielle Giffords, the US congresswoman from Arizona who had been shot and suffered a brain injury. He admires her tenacity and toughness. The name seemed to fit our new puppy, and the nickname Gabby has stuck.

Rebecca had several more corrective ankle surgeries and continued to improve. We felt we were all on the road to recovery. By the spring of 2012, our hospital visits had slowed. Chuck and I were ready to take that trip to Boston and Cape Cod to see what we could find. Our terrific travel agent put everything back into place and dates were set for May 2012.

Looking back at this time in our lives, I reflect on the notion that each of us has an amazing wealth of inner strength to just keep going. No matter what is thrown at us. I had witnessed this strength in my own parents as they dealt with all that life gave them. They moved forward and never looked back.

Just maybe I have some of that inner strength and don't always recognize it. We always have the option of giving up—or trying to reorganize our family system and move forward. Systems fascinate me, and our family system had been nudged big-time. Serious illnesses do that, to all of us. Systems regroup and reorganize—and so did we.

I had also learned that this inner strength needs to have care and nurture. Almost losing my true love made me realize the gifts of today. Family and friendships became more precious. If we could find out more about Col. Taylor, that would be icing on our family cake. Of course, I wanted to find more puzzle pieces and get enough icing to cover the whole cake! But maybe the little bit we already knew about Chuck's father would be enough.

15

Visit to Cape Cod and Boston

*I*n May of 2012, Chuck and I boarded the jet for Boston. We had our folders of information about Col. Taylor carefully tucked away in our carry-on luggage. We had maps and booklets about Cape Cod and Boston. We also had the unknown facing us.

Several years prior to this trip, Chuck and I had traveled to Boston and the surrounding historical sites. We explored the typical tourist visiting destinations: Providence, Rhode Island; the *Mayflower*; the Freedom Trail; and Concord. We had walked the streets of Boston and felt the history all around us. It was thrilling for both of us to be returning. But this time the agenda was very different.

Because of the time difference between the West Coast and the East Coast, we arrived late in the afternoon. A few hours after deplaning we were in our medium-sized rental car heading to Cape Cod. The afternoon light slowly began to fade as we approached. We circumvented the maze of narrow tree-lined streets and made our way into the village of Sandwich. After a few wrong turns, we arrived at our lodging at the Dan'l Webster Inn. The inn had been named after Daniel Webster, an early American patriot born in 1782 who grew up as our young country was forming. He was known for his oratory skills. Since we were searching for our history, it seemed fitting to be staying in an early-American traditional two-storied wooden clapboard house. It was painted a deep red with black shutters at the windows. Against the early evening darkness, we could see the entrance. It was like a beacon of light shining out a welcome.

We retrieved our luggage and walked in. There was the immediate smell of old house, in a good way. It felt like going back in time. We were greeted by friendly staff and given directions to our room. Our travel agent knew us well. She had requested that we have a room in the old, original part of the inn. There were no elevators, so we walked up wide wooden stairs with a runner carpet. We could hear the creak of the wooden floors in the hallway as we walked to our room. The room was immaculate and elegantly decorated with a fireplace. It had a huge four-poster bed with a lace canopy and blue floral dust ruffle. The same blue floral print was used for the curtains and two overstuffed wingback chairs. This would be a lovely home for the next few days. After a long day of travel, both of us let out a sigh of relief that we were there.

We were starving and ready for dinner. The inn had a beautiful wood-paneled bar pub with lantern-like lights that just reeked of age and history. It didn't take us long to decide on one of our most favorite dinners: juicy burgers with steak fries and, of course, ale on tap. We were seated at a small table with a party of older women next to us. I can remember that as we sat there taking in our surroundings, I could hear much of the women's conversation.

They were quietly chatting about their gardens and getting their vegetables started soon after the last frost. This was so foreign to me! We lived in sunny Southern California; fruits and vegetables abound all year long. This small snippet of conversation made me realize the differences of place and time.

Our internal clocks were on a different time, but we were ready to settle in. Our plans for the next day included going to the cemetery. I'm sure my head hit the pillow wondering what the next few days would tell us.

After a big breakfast in the pub, we headed out with our maps and files about Charlie. It was a beautiful day with crystal clear skies and a light breeze. Chuck's excellent navigational skills had us driving into the cemetery entrance within minutes. I can remember thinking, *This is where Col. Taylor is buried along with other soldiers who have served our country.* Military cemeteries have a reverence and quiet unlike other cemeteries. Knowing that all of these soldiers had given so much to defend our freedoms was overwhelming. The man or woman under each stone has a life story to tell. All those soldiers had come together for the common purpose of defending our country.

The signage took us to a side-by-side trailer which was being used as the temporary information center. Construction was underway for a new center and museum. We quietly opened the door and stepped into the room. Immediately we were greeted with: "How can we help you?" The room was crowded with desks, files, cabinets, and a few workers. As we entered, we saw a desk sideways to the front door. A younger-looking man with regular street clothes, no uniform, sat behind the desk. I somehow expected that everyone would be in uniform. We just stood there and began to explain. Where to begin?

Chuck said that we were looking for his father's grave site. He gave an abbreviated version of our story. As he shared about finding the letters, the DD 214s, and the death certificate, another gentleman came closer to the desk and started listening in. They seemed intrigued by the story.

They immediately got us a map of the cemetery and showed us where the marker was. They told us that everybody working in these offices is former military, now in civilian roles. They were very friendly. As we started to leave, one gentleman asked Chuck if he had anything to leave at the grave site. This had never occurred to us.

He suggested, "Maybe even a coin that you could wedge down around the grave marker. It would probably be good to leave something of yourself."

What an insightful idea, and a simple gesture of kindness to offer it. I think he could feel our emotions and our desire to find Chuck's father.

We drove around and around. I think cemeteries are planned and landscaped to add interest. You don't just see squared off blocks, but small areas plotted around a hill or tree or hedge. This cemetery was no different. The streets had names like Veterans Way, Patriot Lane, Lexington Circle, and Concord Lane. We arrived on Concord Lane in front of Section 25. Very slowly we walked through, with gravestones all around us, looking for Site 540.

There it was.

We just stood staring down at the stone: "Charles Edward Taylor." The silence was like nothing I had ever heard before—an emptiness of time and space. Tears immediately started rolling down my cheeks. I felt a satisfaction for helping to bring Chuck to this place, but the emotion was fleeting. Yes, we knew the vital information like birth date and death date. Our research had given us a few hints into the decorated life Col. Taylor had lived in the military. What we *didn't* know was the sound of his laughter or his smile. My emotions slipped into sadness and anger at *all the moments lost* between father and son.

Chuck slowly knelt down in front of the stone. He began to clean it off. He pulled the bits of grass that had grown over the edges and gently brushed away the leaves. I was certainly tuned in to his silence. This was not a time to talk or process our feelings. We just took in the moment. Our hearts and minds filled with questions and what-ifs . . .

The gentlemen at the information center had also suggested that we might want to do a pencil printing. Fortunately, among our files we had blank paper and always a pencil. I sat down next to the gravestone and carefully laid the blank paper over the words. As my pencil moved back and forth the words came into focus.

CHARLES EDWARD TAYLOR

July 18, 1918 – November 23, 1997

KEEP 'EM FLYING DAD

WE LOVE YOU AND MISS YOU

Once I had finished the print, Chuck began to look for a coin that he could wedge between the ground and the stone. He carefully took out all of his change and I searched my purse too. There were a few quarters. Chuck looked at the dates on each one and chatted about any relevance to these dates. There didn't seem to be any connections. I think he ended up choosing the one closest to our coming to the cemetery. He placed the coin in the top right side of the gravestone and pushed and pushed. Maybe each push was saying, "I'm here."

180

As we began to think about leaving, we noticed an empty grave site right next to Charlie's grave. There were no other empty plots. What did this mean? The news article about Col. Taylor's appendicitis attack had given us a Mrs. Charles Taylor, and the death certificate named the spouse as Carol Swiss. Could this site be waiting for her? Was she still alive? Our curiosity had us returning to the information center.

As we entered the second time, the gentlemen were interested in hearing about our success in finding the grave. We thanked them for their suggestions and shared about our leaving a coin.

Then we asked about the empty grave site. "Is that site for Mrs. Taylor?" We told them about the appendicitis attack. The newspaper article had quoted Mrs. Taylor, which put her in Russia with Col. Taylor.

The protocol for giving information on someone who has not passed away didn't allow them to verify who had reserved that grave site. But very casually, the two gentlemen walked a few feet away and opened a file drawer. They pulled the file for that grave site. The two men then had a conversation that was loud enough for us to hear. The file confirmed that this site was for Mrs. Taylor. It was an obvious action to give us the information we wanted but did not violate protocol. We never *saw* the file; we just "accidentally" overheard a conversation between two coworkers.

As we drove away, our thoughts and emotions were on overload. We had stood at the grave site of Chuck's father and cried. We felt some closure in finding Charlie. But a new door had opened. Where was Mrs. Taylor? Could we find the obituary?

The rest of the day was spent driving around exploring a small area of Cape Cod. Both of us enjoy Boston-style clam chowder, so our mission for the rest of the day was a leisurely drive to find a spot known for its chowder. Unfortunately, we were visiting in the off-season. Summer was just around the corner, but many vacation restaurants were not yet open. We never did find that clam chowder. Even though the weather was bright and sunny, our brains remained in a kind of fog.

As I look back, I think this was a transition day for our emotions. We had found Charlie's grave site. We knew he had had a long, successful life—seventy-nine years. We could decide to stop our journey here. Just go home and be satisfied with knowing the little we knew.

But we didn't do that. The letters from the closet still held secrets. Once the ribbon had been untied, we knew we had to keep going. We had more to discover.

Gravestone of Col. Charles Edward Taylor. Massachusetts National Cemetery. Chuck and Ann saw the gravestone for the first time in 2012.

The Ribbon Untied

16

Somerville Library: More Secrets

*T*he morning after visiting the cemetery we slept in. We knew we would be fighting the Boston rush-hour traffic, so having a leisurely morning seemed the best idea.

On our previous trip to Boston, we had discovered Dunkin' Donuts. This was not a "thing" in California, and Chuck and I both really like donuts. Leaving the Dan'l Webster Inn, we were on a mission to find the closest Dunkin' Donuts. It didn't take long before we walked in the door with the sweet smell of sugar hitting us in the face. Like kids in a candy store, we did our usual overindulgence. We chose maple bars, chocolate bars, cinnamon, and plain raised. With orders of coffee and a bag of sweets, we headed for the Somerville library.

Again, we were armed with our research and documents. The death certificate had indicated that Somerville was the last place Col. Taylor had lived. If there was an obituary, it seemed logical that the *Somerville Times* newspaper would be the place to search. When I searched for Mary Lou's family, it was the obituary of one of Chuck's cousins that opened the door. We were hoping we might have similar success finding someone on the Taylor side of the family.

Somerville is a city just two miles north of Boston. It was settled in 1630 as part of Charlestown. (Seems fitting since we were looking for Charles Taylor.) It has grown into a very diverse, bustling community that boasts important involvement in the birth of our country. During the American Revolution, it was the site of critical military positions. The "Midnight Ride of Paul Revere" went through Somerville (Charlestown). Most notably, Prospect Hill is the site of the raising of the first Grand Union Flag on orders of General George Washington on January 1, 1776.

The layout of the city is defined by its squares. The neighborhood boundaries have their own unique personalities. The big trees lining the narrow streets had just put out their springtime leaves that rustled in the breeze. Lots of cars were parked on the streets because very few houses have garages.

Our maps and GPS had us pulling up in front of the Somerville Public Library. The slightly tattered sign was surrounded by early spring flowers. The library was an older building and much like the Dan'l Webster Inn. It had the smell of an old building filled with books but was very comforting. The wooden steps creaked as we walked up to the entrance. A friendly receptionist greeted us and pointed us to the microfiche section on the second floor.

This library brought back memories of my childhood library adventures. My brother and I would ride the city bus that passed directly in front of our house to a bus stop across the street from the library. He and I would climb the steps of on old church that had been turned into the library. The original stained-glass windows let in filtered light as shadows danced across the old wooden floors. It smelled of books and highly polished wood. The children's section was on the second floor, which had probably been the choir loft of the church. We two kids would wander, pick out books, sit, and read until we had chosen just the right ones. The crowded stacks were always intriguing and a bit scary. All those stories just waiting to be read! Why does everyone always whisper?

This memory flashed before me as Chuck and I headed up another set of stairs. Before entering the microfiche section, we had to be approved by a library staff member at a big wooden counter. I recall that the gentleman who helped us was intrigued by our request. The fact that we had come all the way from California was certainly unusual. We briefly told him the story and what we were looking for: obituary records for Col. Taylor. To be able to use the equipment and the microfiche files, we had to give him a driver's license. I quickly handed over mine.

The file drawers and cabinets seemed bunched together with very little space to work. An older gentleman sat at one of the machines. We wedged our way into the small table and chairs and started scanning the organizational system. The files were by dates. We knew the death date, November 23, 1997. We assumed that if there was an obituary, it would follow this date. We began with November 24, then 25, pulling each file out and loading it into the microfiche machine. On to November 26, 27, 28, 29, 30. Wouldn't an obituary be posted within a week of someone's passing? But we found nothing.

My disappointment started to edge in. We had come so far! Was there any other resource to use?

The man next to us seemed very focused and busy, but Chuck interrupted him and asked his advice about other possible newspapers. The man told us that he was looking for Civil War veterans who had lived in Somerville. Since Memorial Day was coming soon, the local historical association was hoping to showcase some of these veterans. We quickly told him our story. And without any hesitation he suggested looking in the *Boston Globe*.

"Where is that located?" Chuck asked.

"Right behind you on that wall," he said.

We turned around to find a huge set of files that encompassed the news from the world-renowned *Boston Globe*. With a sliver of hope we found the appropriate dates.

On November 25, 1997, there it was.

TAYLOR-Of Somerville, Nov. 23, Colonel Charles E. Husband of Carol Taylor of Somerville. Father of James Taylor of Deerfield, MA, Maile Roper of Biddeford, ME, Jane Taylor of Somerville, and Marcia Taylor Zinno of Providence, RI. He is also survived by 8 grandchildren. A Memorial Service will be held Saturday, Nov. 29, at 10 a.m. in the Church of the Good Shepherd, Watertown. (617)-924-9420 Relatives and friends are invited to attend. Visiting hours omitted. Burial private. Memorial contributions can be made in Charles' memory to the Alzheimers Assoc., GRECC Unit, Veterans Administration Hospital, Bedford, MA 01730. Arrangements by the Cremation Society of Mass., 1-800-696-5887.

Obituary of Col. Charles Edward Taylor, posted in the *Boston Globe*, 1997.

I don't think I have words to describe our emotions. There, in black-and-white—*a whole family* that we never knew existed! We both read and reread.

The Ribbon Untied

Chuck probably had some words like, "Holy *shit!* I have a *family!*" I probably laughed a slightly nervous laugh, which I do when I don't have words to attach to my emotions. Chuck whipped out his camera and took a picture of the file. Then we sent the file to the copy machine. This would give us an immediate copy to add to the treasure of records. I think we turned to the gentleman and told him we had found it, but I can't be sure. We tidied up our work space, put everything back, pushed in our chairs, and nearly skipped out of the library into the bright sun.

We wound our way out of Somerville and headed to the interstate highway to return to Cape Cod. I'm sure our heads were spinning, but we did very little talking.

About forty-five minutes into our journey, we received a phone call from Rebecca in California. She'd been contacted by someone from the Somerville library. "Mom, you left your driver's license at the desk there." The microfiche library staff person had tracked her down! He still had my license and used the information on it—along with his library skills and resources—to locate our daughter. I was so glad we had shared some of the family story with him because he was able to figure it all out. Without that license, I wouldn't be able to board the plane the next day. The gods were with us!

The next freeway exit had us turning back toward Somerville. I quickly retrieved my license. The librarian who had helped us was gone for the day, but I left my very big thanks with his coworker.

Since we knew the traffic going through Boston would be horrific, we decided to wander in Somerville awhile. We had the address on the death certificate. Would we be able to find the house where Chuck's father lived? What if Mrs. Taylor still lived there?

We meandered through narrow streets lined with row houses made of clapboard and some of brick. Many of the houses seemed to be duplexes with a shared front porch. We found the house, 2 Campbell Park. It looked like most of the others. The streets were filled with parked cars; no signs of anyplace to pull over. We drove slowly up and down several times just looking, our emotions swirling. We certainly didn't want to seem like we were casing the place.

Our ride back to Cape Cod had moments of quiet and then a burst and repeat of "Oh, my gosh!" or "Holy shit, I have a family!" Then the question, "Who are these people?"

Finally, we reached the Dan'l Webster Inn. Somehow it seemed to offer comfort as we drove up and headed for our room. We were emotionally and physically exhausted! We sat up in that big four-poster bed with the fancy canopy. We leaned back on the big fluffy pillows, stretched out our legs, and let out a very big exhale!

What had we uncovered?

We opened the file with our papers. On the very top was the copy of the obituary. Carol Taylor was still living. There was a brother, a sister, another sister, and then another sister! After each name was their city of residence. Not only did we have names, we had *places*.

The what-ifs just started to tumble out. I think Chuck was imagining all these siblings being one big happy "Norman Rockwell Family." Again, he was on the outside looking in. We knew about them, but they didn't have any clues about Chuck and his family. We read and reread the obituary. Siblings with the names James, Maile, Jane, and Marcia. Then there were eight grandchildren. We sat for a long time just trying to absorb our discovery. The light faded in the room and our

188

stomachs began to growl. It had been a *long time* since we'd had those donuts!

The cozy pub at the inn was a welcome place to enjoy fish and chips. Chuck and I talked and talked, reliving the last few days. There were the wonders of finding family and all the questions still ahead.

We had brought to Cape Cod file folders filled with information about Col. Taylor. We were returning to California with those same folders—but now they were filled with information about a family that Chuck never knew he had. Would Chuck choose to try to find his family of siblings? Only he could make that decision.

17

The Siblings: Who Are These Guys?

All those names in the obituary. Who were they? I am a visual learner and can conjure up vivid images in my head when I think of my family. I didn't have a picture in my head of any of Chuck's siblings. They were just names—James, Maile, Jane, and Marcia. Would Chuck want to pursue the quest of finding them? Could we put faces with those names? These questions bounced around in my head as we flew across the country, headed home to California.

Chuck seemed to be energized about trying to make contact with his siblings. Hopefully, we could find them all. He continued to wonder out loud about the amazing find in the obituary. We shared this excitement with our daughters and our friends. It was like all of us being in a mystery or treasure hunt trying to piece together the clues.

The feelings of hope were also accompanied with questions about acceptance or rejection. Chuck would say, "What if they do not acknowledge me?" "What if they acknowledge me but do not want to tell me anything?" "What if Mrs. Carol Taylor is still alive? Will she know anything?" "Do I try to contact her?" "What if they are a big Norman Rockwell Family, and my presence on the scene is very troubling to them?" "Do I want to take a chance of disrupting the family?"

Every time we'd discuss whether to move forward, these doubts would surface. What were the risks of moving forward? Could finding the family be more important than possibly hurting the family? Chuck had to make the decision.

He wanted to know about his father, and finding family members would be a bonus. Over the course of several weeks, Chuck decided that knowing about his family was worth the possibility of being rejected. It was worth going forward—no matter what the outcome.

Now that the decision was made, I began the task of locating places of residence—finding the address of each new sibling. My sleuthing skills were itching to get back to work to locate these new people in our lives. Also, *time* seemed to be a factor in our thinking. We had missed knowing Chuck's father by a few years. We didn't want to wait too long and miss the chance to connect.

Researching family members through computer sites such as ancestry.com was no longer helpful. I had to figure out how to locate *living* people. My tech skills are not the best, so this was difficult and tedious. I relied on my jigsaw-puzzle methods. Look for big pieces and try to make connections. However, there were many starts and dead ends until I figured out the systems.

Computer sites exist that are much like the old "white pages" of the phone books. These sites also show connections to other family members. This is where I landed for my search. Since the obituary had given the name of a town or city for each sibling, I was able to narrow my search. Once again, I ran into the problem of Taylor being a very common name. There are gazillions of James Taylors and Jane Taylors and Marcia Taylors! The name that was the linchpin for me was Maile Roper. Because it's such a distinctive name, I could use her name to cross-reference the others. Internet "white pages" would also give me the names of possible relatives along with addresses. So, finding Maile had me going back again and again to the many Taylors to look for the other siblings.

Over many days of searching, I was able to zero in on an address for each of the four siblings. At least that is what I told myself. I couldn't be sure. For example, Marcia Taylor was also listed as Marcia Zinno. Was this a married name? Where did Marcia Taylor live? I shared my progress with Chuck, and he helped make the final decisions about the likely accuracy of the addresses. All we had to lose was a letter going to someone who may not be related—or someone who chose to ignore Chuck's letter.

The next task was very difficult: how to introduce ourselves to Chuck's siblings. We didn't want them to think we were *kooks* just trying to horn in on their family. We had to show that we were legitimate.

The letter needed to be in Chuck's voice because the story was coming from him reaching out to new family members. We spent many conversations discussing what to say and what to include. Chuck wanted to show his family connection and extend a hand of possibly getting to know them. Do we send any of the letters from Charlie to Mary Lou? The letters and the DD 214s showed Charlie's signature. Did they need to be included as proof? Also, should we send Chuck's birth certificate with Charles Edward Taylor, Jr.? Do we include any of the facts we have uncovered—the appendicitis in Russia, Charlie's plane going down and being rescued by the *Razorback* submarine, the death certificate, the DD 214s?

Ultimately, we decided that I would write a draft of the letter and include everything we knew to date. Then Chuck would rewrite it and make it his own.

Dear James, Maile, Jane and Marcia,

This may be one of the most unusual letters you have ever received. It was a challenge for me to write and introduce myself to you all—I believe I am your half brother and that we share the same father.

After the opening paragraph, the letter went on for two-plus pages. There were details about finding the letters to Mary Lou from Chas; our search for Chas, Charlie, Col. Taylor; what we discovered about Col. Taylor and his military service; and ultimately finding the obituary, which led us to each of the siblings.

Chuck closed the letter so beautifully:

I have tried to imagine receiving a letter such as this. I can't. I hope it does not cause any of you or your mother (should you share it with her) pain. For me there was no way I could not send it. Please know I would really love to talk to any or all of you.

Included in the envelope would be copies of the first and last letters to Mary Lou and the birth certificate. We also decided to send two pictures of Col. Taylor and one of ourselves taken at a pub in New York a few years back.

How could we show them who we are? After much thought we decided to include a letter that introduced us, our family, and our professional lives. We laughed about wanting to be seen as real and stable—*not* kooks.

We put all of this together: Chuck's letter of introduction, the two letters from Charlie, our letter about us, and pictures. As with so many other decisions we'd made around finding Chuck's family, we needed our good friends Margee and Bill to weigh in. They had invited us over for dinner on Memorial Day.

We wanted them to look at what we'd written with an eye for what to expect. If they had ever received this type of communication, what would they do? Had we worded it with sensitivity and included legitimate information?

Seated around Margee and Bill's huge kitchen island over appetizers, gin and tonics, and wine, we shared our plan and our letters. An added bonus was having Margee's mother, Evelyn, join us for dinner. Since my mother had died in 2004, Evelyn had been like a mother to me. She loved Chuck and me, and we always enjoyed hearing her stories and understanding her perspective.

Interestingly, Evelyn had been a young bride around the time that Charlie and Mary Lou had been together—1941 through 1944. Evelyn had insights into the world of that time, particularly about young people going off to war. What would they be doing and thinking? Chuck and I had been somewhat judgmental about Charlie leaving Mary Lou. But Evelyn shared that young soldiers never knew if they were going to make it to another day. In her own gentle way, she encouraged us not to be too hard on Charlie.

Chuck and I sat patiently as the letters were passed around among Bill, Margee, and Evelyn. All of them knew the story in bits and pieces, as we had told it many times. But this was the first time they had seen the whole story laid out with a chronology and

The Ribbon Untied

supporting information. Did the letters make sense? What needed more clarification? What needed to be taken out?

We all sat and talked. I don't recall any major suggestions for revision, but I do remember a strong sense of support for sending the letters, no matter what the consequences. It was a fun, laughter-filled evening with dear friends.

Chuck also sent our draft letter to our other good friends, Rich and Gayle. Rich and Chuck had worked together for years and were best buddies. They retired within a year of each other and began working on major home projects. For our home, they designed and rebuilt a stone fireplace, remodeled our bar area, and completely remade a bathroom. At Gayle and Rich's house, they removed the cottage cheese ceiling and repainted. Gayle even had special T-shirts made that said *Endless Summer Remodeling*. Their days were filled with hard work, lots of laughter, and usually a turkey sandwich from Jersey Mike's Subs. Two retired guys having a fun time.

Hearing Rich's thoughts about this letter was important to Chuck. Rich's response was extremely positive and encouraging about moving forward to find Chuck's family.

Our team of friends had given us support. Even if the new family never materialized, we had this family of loving friends.

In early June we put the finishing touches on the letters, added our phone numbers, and prepared them for mailing. We used large white envelopes, printed each name with care, and included the return address in the upper left-hand corner. At the post office we registered each envelope so we would know when it was delivered. Off they went!

Afterwards, we celebrated with chocolate mint ice cream for me, and coffee malt with extra coffee syrup for Chuck. A weight had been lifted off our shoulders. But an anxiety settled in about whether any response might come back, and if it did, what it might be.

The postal system could give us an approximate date of delivery. We mailed the letters on June 6, and we could expect them to arrive June 9 or 10. For a few days, all we could do was hope the letters arrived. Cell phones were not as attached to our hips as they are today, but Chuck had included his cell number on the letter as a point of contact. After day two of waiting, he kept the cell phone with him at all times—just in case someone called.

Over the next three days, Chuck and I tried to keep to our regular schedule. I had finished the semester of teaching but had to wrap up some paperwork. We took extra-long walks with the dog every day, and Chuck was always busy with his photography. We tried not to dwell on waiting to hear from a new family member, but I know it was always in the back of our minds. We had never been in this position of facing so much that was unknown. It was certainly a time of quiet anxiety for me—anticipating results. Even if we never heard back from any of Chuck's family, I had to be satisfied that what we had learned to date would be enough. But I know in my heart that I wanted so much more for Chuck.

Chuck had tried to keep his cell phone with him, but on day three he sat the phone down next to his computer and accidentally left it there. I am often the first one in bed, and Chuck putters around before he settles in. He had gone into his office to put his phone in the charger. There was a flashing message. A number he didn't recognize. Next thing I knew he was leaning over me on the bed as I was dozing off. "Listen to this. A message from my sister!"

Clear as day, I heard, "Welcome to the family, Brother. Hope we can talk soon. Maile."

The first call—one of warmth and welcome!

Chuck and I were giddy. How exciting to have such a call! Of course, now we were wide awake. No sleep for many hours; just talking and feeling awash with emotions. With Gabby asleep in her crate and our two cats cuddled around our legs, we just sat in the middle of our big bed and talked over comfort food snacks. It could have been popcorn or ice cream or Oreos and milk. We wouldn't have known or remembered.

We recreated and rehashed the events of the last year trying to take in our adventures. From June 2011 when I gave Chuck the book about his father to now, June 2012, our world of family had changed. We had gone from assuming Chuck's father had died in World War II when Chuck was a child to knowing that Charlie had lived to the age of seventy-nine and had a family. Chuck had gone from being an only child to having siblings.

I continued to be touched by the gift of letters from Charlie to Mary Lou. These letters tied in the red ribbon, continuing to give. I'm not sure what Mary Lou would have thought, but she kept the letters for a reason. I think she loved Charlie very much and wanted her only son to have just a small piece of his father. We weren't sure where the next chapter of this saga would lead, but we were so very glad we chose to send those letters to Chuck's siblings.

18

Getting to Know the Sibs

*C*huck was up early to make the call to his newfound sister, Maile. Since she lived in Minnesota, there was a time difference to consider. As he called, I could feel the butterflies in my stomach. What would she tell him about the family?

When Chuck connected with Maile, a new door opened in his life. I could immediately feel the warmth and hear the laughter as she and Chuck said hello to each other for the first time. Chuck was sitting in the big lounge chair in our room, and I was perched on the bed. His face beamed as they talked.

She shared that she had almost thrown away the envelope. Maile and her medical assistant were going through the huge stack of mail on the first day back in the clinic after a vacation. Being a doctor, she gets lots of advertisements and letters from companies trying to sell her their products. Maile picked up one envelop after another. The big white envelope looked much like many others. But her assistant noticed that it had been hand addressed. Maybe it wasn't like the others, and she encouraged Maile to open it.

What a surprise!

As Maile tells the story, she yelled out, "Holy shit—I have another *brother*!" Her voice echoed down the hall to other offices, and soon colleagues came running. With her staff around her she read the letters and looked at the pictures. Maile was then very quick to put in calls to her other siblings—James, Jane, and Marcia. They had not received their envelopes yet. Talk about news spreading like wildfire! I can only imagine the conversations as she told her brother and sisters what had just arrived.

Chuck and Maile talked for over an hour. The conversation was filled with revelations about Chuck's father. Maile shared that Col. Taylor (Chas, Charlie, Dad) had married her mother, Marguerite, in Hawaii. James was Maile's older brother. After a few years of marriage, Charlie and Marguerite divorced. Charlie had stayed in the service and was sent to Michigan State University to study foreign relations and Russian. There he met Carol and they later married. Along came Jane and then Marcia.

This first conversation put the idea of the "Norman Rockwell Family" to rest. At first blush, this was a family structure like many other families. I was filled with so many emotions: excitement, gratitude that she had called, pleased with our success in finding them, and anticipation about everything and anything we would learn.

Over the next twenty-four hours, Chuck received a call from each of his siblings! Each one was warm and welcoming. There were long conversations about how the family all fits together. It was like drinking from a firehose. So much information and new family dynamics were being shared. And if that weren't enough, both of Charlie's wives were still alive.

Chuck's brother James (or Jim, as they call him) had some of the most interesting and shocking information to share. Jim was born in August of 1944, just *two months after Chuck*. But the letters from Charlie to Mary Lou continued after Chuck was born, until October 1944. The family story was that Marguerite and Charlie had met at a party, and once she knew she was pregnant, her brothers "gently forced" Charlie to marry her. Jim described it as a shotgun wedding.

After we learned from Jim about how his father married Marguerite, I wondered if this was the information that Mary Lou had shared with James Ballou back in 1945. James had sent this response to Mary Lou:

> *I got your letter post-marked 25 April today. It said what I was afraid it would say. However, I will say this about Slug, Sr., he is a pretty intelligent gent even if he is a very spoiled little boy. If Slug gets the training his old man so obviously needed and missed he might be quite a boy at that.*

Jim also told Chuck that after Charlie and Marguerite divorced, Marguerite took the two children, Jim and Maile, and moved to Kansas. There she met and married a man named Blanton. Three more children were added to the mix. So, James and Maile had half siblings Harriet (Hat), Diedre (Dee), and Buzz. All of these half and stepsiblings considered themselves part of the family. Chuck had gone from having four half siblings to having an additional three stepsiblings, for a total of seven new siblings from the Taylor/Blanton blended family. With Chuck, the magic number of siblings in the family became eight.

Jane was able to tell Chuck about the last years and final days of his father's life. Charlie and wife Carol (Jane's mom) had moved with Jane to Somerville, Massachusetts. Originally, Carol and Charlie shared a duplex with Jane. But when Charlie started to decline with memory problems, Carol and Charlie moved out of their unit and into Jane's. Charlie spent the last few months of his life in a veterans hospital in Bedford, Massachusetts. Jane shared that Carol now lived in a senior home and was still very independent.

Jane was a practicing public health nurse in the Boston area and had built a home in central Massachusetts on seventy acres of protected forestland. She was hoping to retire soon and move permanently to her new home.

Marcia was the youngest Taylor. She taught music in a Quaker school in Providence, Rhode Island. Marcia wrote music, sang, and played the guitar, and she had several recordings to her credit. Since Chuck loves folk music, this was an immediate connection.

Jim had served in the navy for many years. Once he was discharged, life offered some fascinating career options. He was a professional portrait painter and artist, and showed some of his work in galleries on the East Coast. In the winter he worked as a professional Santa Claus. He was also renewing his relationship with a high school sweetheart, Jean, in North Carolina. Jean is the twin sister of Jim's best friend in Kansas.

This was an exciting, stimulating time for Chuck as he began to build these new relationships. But he only knew these siblings through their *voices*. Almost all of us who have siblings know them through so much more than voices. We know their smiles, their habits, the way they walk and run, their anger, and their laughter—their sneezes! We have been teased, pinched, pulled and punched, hugged and kissed by our siblings. Chuck had none of these experiences. He was starting at ground zero in knowing a new brother and three sisters, plus the additional family. He might *imagine* what his brother and sisters looked like, but for now, he was learning about them through their voices.

After the initial phone calls from all the siblings, the next few months of 2012 were filled with more conversations. Jim and Chuck seemed to connect the most, maybe as brothers in this field of sisters. One day I stood at the doorway and just watched and listened as Chuck made his first FaceTime call—to Jim. This was a historic moment between the two brothers, a leap from just hearing Jim's voice to seeing his face! Chuck knew from previous calls that Jim had been a professional Santa Claus, so it wasn't surprising to see his rounded, gray-bearded face appear on the screen. Jim's voice matches the image of a jolly Santa, deep and clear. The two just stared and laughed as they said hello in person—face-to-face! Two brothers just two months apart.

Almost immediately, Jim said to Chuck, "Turn sideways. Turn sideways—I want to see your profile." And then, quietly, he said, "*So* Dad!"

This was Chuck's time to take it all in. I was thrilled to witness his excitement from a distance. At this point I think I probably lost it, quietly crying with joy as I listened to two brothers see each other for the first time.

In retrospect, Chuck and I were living in the moment of finding new family. We were thoroughly enjoying the mystery and intrigue, seeing it from our eyes only. I have often wondered what his brother and sisters must have thought about their father after we entered the scene. The Taylor kids had grown up knowing Marguerite and Charlie's relationship, then Carol and Charlie's relationship. This was their combined history. But all of a sudden, this strange letter appears, and their father has a dimension they did not know about. They could easily have said, no thanks, we're not interested. But thank God, they didn't!

The letters from Charlie that Mary Lou had kept hidden in her closet were the source of a whole new world for Chuck. Untying that ribbon led us to an amazing life-changing gift: the gift of a family who threw open the doors of their hearts and let us in!

CHRONOLOGY OF TAYLOR SIBLING BIRTHS

September 1943	**Lt. Mary Lou Haines and Maj. Charles Taylor spend a leave together at Kilauea Military Camp, Hawaii.**
–	
April 1944	**Marriage of Marguerite Willett and Charles Taylor**
–	
June 24, 1944	Chuck born to Mary Lou Haines and Charles Taylor
–	
August 25, 1944	James Taylor born to Marguerite and Charles Taylor
October 23, 1946	Maile Taylor born to Marguerite and Charles Taylor
–	
September 3, 1949	**Marriage of Carol Swiss and Charles Taylor**
November 5, 1950	Jane Taylor born to Carol and Charles Taylor
June 3, 1953	Marcia Taylor born to Carol and Charles Taylor

19

Meeting Niece Tilly

*A*s Chuck and Jim began to talk and FaceTime call in the fall of 2012, Jim shared about his own life. He had been married previously and had a daughter, Tilly, and a son, Khalil. In just the past year, Jim had left Massachusetts and moved to North Carolina to renew his friendship with his high school sweetheart. Tilly was attending the Massachusetts Institute of Technology (MIT) and was on the track team as a javelin thrower. Khalil was still in high school and lived with his mother in central Massachusetts, just a few miles from Jane's home.

In early spring 2013, Jim called Chuck to tell him that Tilly was heading to California to compete in a track meet. Would we be able to go see her? I think Chuck would have traveled a long distance to make this connection. But as it happened, the meet was at a university in Santa Barbara, just about an hour from our home. We were both thrilled to meet her.

We arrived early to get the lay of the land. The weather was picture perfect with blue skies and a gentle breeze coming off the

Pacific Ocean. Most track meets gather athletes from multiple schools, and this was no different. We walked all around the perimeter of the field and track. We could see tents and canopies being erected for each school. We were looking for the MIT team. Student teams were starting to arrive, set up their gear, and practice.

Chuck had made arrangements through Jim to connect with Tilly by phone. We wanted to see if we could identify who she was before Chuck called her. Having been a high school principal, Chuck had attended many track meets, so he was familiar with how the events were laid out. We found the javelin area and saw athletes warming up. We didn't know what Tilly looked like, but the students wore uniforms that distinguished each school. There were several women out practicing, and we thought we could identify Tilly in her MIT shirt of deep burgundy and gray.

Chuck made the call to let Tilly know we had arrived. We planned to meet her briefly before the competition.

"Hi, Tilly, we're here. We are standing at the opposite end from your javelin competition, just outside the track on the other side of the fence. I have on a baseball cap and a plaid shirt, and Ann has on a straw sun hat. I also have my camera." Very quickly, she was right in front of us.

The hellos were a bit awkward, but smiles of joy covered all our faces! Here in this most unlikely place was Chuck's first visit with *a living relative* on his father's side!

We chatted very briefly and asked Tilly if she'd be able to leave after her competition and join us for lunch in Santa Barbara. She said she would have to ask her coach. We agreed to meet her in the same spot after the competition. We told her we would be in the stands cheering her on. Quick good-byes and good luck, and she trotted off to the other end of the field to warm up.

Chuck and I hurried into the stands to get as close as we could to see her compete. I had never seen the javelin throw, so it was intriguing to watch. Each athlete took multiple steps to build energy into their body and arms before they hurled the javelin. Officials and spotters in the field measure and record each throw. Each athlete made three throws, with the longest distance being their score.

Tilly was in the middle of the group of competitors. Chuck began clicking away with his camera when Tilly was next up. Chuck and I had only just met Tilly, but I remember the feeling I used to have when our daughters were competing or performing; this feeling of being so proud, but the butterflies in the stomach and a bit anxious for their success.

Tilly stepped up to the line to begin. We watched the javelin leave her hand and fly into the sky! It came down quickly and stuck into the ground. It all happened very fast.

Tilly seemed to do well, but the final scores would be posted later. Chuck and I hurried down the bleachers and found our way back to the spot to meet Tilly again.

The place was like a beehive as athletes moved from one place to another for their individual sport. Track meets are very different from other sporting events. There are cheers and excited cries at different places around the track and field. Multiple events are going on concurrently. Track and field events are often solitary sports. It seems that the athlete is competing for himself or herself to improve. The joy seems to come in that self-improvement. The team element is supporting each other to better your time or distance or jump.

It was fun to see this part of Tilly's world. We had no frame of reference for knowing her younger life, but being part of this moment was definitely worthwhile.

We didn't have to wait too long before we spotted Tilly heading toward us. I can just see her now. She had a large plastic container of Sabra hummus in her hand and a box of ak-mak crackers under her arm. As she walked to meet us with a big smile, she was taking big bites of cracker piled with hummus. It hit me: she was starving! The students probably have eating schedules to fit in with their strength training and competition cycles.

We stood on opposite sides of the fence and visited. I offered to hold the container of hummus steady as she reached over and scooped with the crackers. Her coach said school policy wouldn't allow her to leave the meet. We certainly understood and respected that decision. We would be satisfied just to visit with her right in that spot.

Chuck asked if she would like to call her dad. Her face lit up! Under the warm California sun, an Uncle Chuck and Niece Tilly made the call.

"Hi Dad, I'm with Uncle Chuck. Ha, Ha—I got to see him first!" Tilly, Chuck, and I had big grins on our faces. We could hear Jim's deep voice say, "Yes, you did." Then his great laugh!

Tilly finished off the hummus as our visit came to an end. We talked about the track meet and asked questions about her competition. She thought she had probably placed third or fourth.

We walked away filled with joy and amazement. Here was this new family member who had traveled across the country to compete in a track meet—that just *happened* to be close to us. Just think about the chances of all of these stars being aligned!

I knew the joy of having aunts and uncles and cousins, and I wanted this for Chuck. And now Chuck's world of connections was expanding—with Tilly—his introduction to his new family.

Tilly Taylor. Competing for Massachusetts Institute of Technology as a javelin thrower in a track meet at Westmont College, Santa Barbara, California, 2013.

The Ribbon Untied

20

Family Reunion

Conversations between Chuck and his siblings continued into the New Year 2013. Over the holidays, Chuck would call or send email greetings to all, just to say hello. We included all of them in our Christmas card and family newsletter. Through all of these phone visits, Jane and Chuck started to discuss having a family reunion.

It's interesting to think about the word *reunion*. It implies that there was a union before. Pieces of a family were bonded together previously, and the desire to reunite creates the common term, family reunion. But this Taylor family gathering would be unique. Here were family members who were known to each other, some connected through their father and others connected as stepsiblings. Then Chuck appears. He has no history with any of these family members.

How does one navigate the emotions and day-to-day feelings of being the newcomer to the party? It seemed to me that Chuck was enjoying the adventure and letting the events unfold.

In the reunion venture, Jane took the lead. She was the master organizer and communicator, pulling it all together. She had enough space in her house to accommodate a few of us. Jane's stepsister Dee, who lived down the drive, had room for several guests too. Everyone was contacted and dates were set for early June.

Chuck and I were both a bit anxious about meeting all of these people. We decided to fly into Boston early and visit the city for a few days before heading to Jane's home. Somehow, we felt the need to take some baby steps before we met everyone. Maybe being in Boston, a city we loved, would help us acclimate.

Just a year before, we had been flying into Boston and heading to Cape Cod, looking for any further clues about Chuck's family. In one short year our world had expanded big-time! It was taking lots of emotional energy to thoughtfully process our feelings about all that had occurred in such a short time.

We planned to spend several days in Boston and be tourists. Cities are always fun for us, as we love to walk and watch and feel the vibrancy of a place. For us, Boston combines the history of its role in the American story, the intellectual hub of so many universities, and the fast pace of modern business. The city seems to thrive from being on the cutting edge of new ideas while holding on to traditions. We spent hours just wandering.

One of the most famous spots is the Boston Commons with its parklike setting, where trees are reflected in the glass of the tall buildings. We were heading to see the memorial that had been spontaneously created for the victims of the Boston Marathon bombing. On this late spring day, there was a light sprinkle of rain, gentle on our faces and probably on our minds. Halfway across the park we stopped on the wide sidewalk to get our bearings. With our heads buried under our hoods, we rechecked the guidebook.

A young thirtyish-looking man approached and asked, "Could I help you find something?"

Chuck asked, "Are we going in the right direction to find the Boston Marathon memorial site?"

He pointed us in the correct direction and asked, "Where are you from?"

We responded, "California."

His friendliness was welcomed and the conversation continued. We noticed he was carrying an instrument case and we asked what he played. He told us that he played a unique Renaissance instrument that was similar to a lute. He was on his way to a rehearsal with a baroque chamber music group.

He sensed our interest. "Would you like to see the instrument?"

"Of course!"

By this time, the misty rain had stopped. And just like that, he put the case on the sidewalk, took out the instrument, and began to play a lyrical tune that floated into the moist air. As he played, another gentleman walked by, recognized the instrument, and stopped to share his appreciation and chat.

What a small serendipitous gift! Within a few minutes we were on our way with smiles and a lighter step. Somehow, this tiny incident seemed to say, "Welcome to the city, and welcome to your family."

Once we reached the memorial site and saw the display of running shoes mixed with people's cards and flowers, our feelings became more sober. It was difficult to view, as we thought about the lives that had been shattered on that fateful day. But we had seen evidence of Boston Strong—from the friendly musician to the public outpouring of love and support for those who had lived through this tragic terrorist attack.

On the way back to our hotel, Chuck got a call from his sister Jane. "Would you be able to stop at MIT tomorrow and pick up Tilly? And bring her to the reunion?" We were flattered to be asked. In that moment it seemed like we were just part of the family—the kind that asks for and offers help to one another.

It was a simple gesture that showed belonging. This was probably a new experience for Chuck. He had seen this in my family, but having this type of acceptance from *his* family was a brand-new experience.

The next day, we rendezvoused with Tilly along the main street of MIT. Tilly settled into the back seat with her sleeping bag and backpack as we drove away, down the wide tree-lined boulevard. She pointed out the buildings on the right and explained that this was "the Humanities School for MIT." Then she laughed and said, "No—that's Harvard!" Chuck tucked that funny comment into his brain to share with our friend Bill, a Harvard grad. To this day, Chuck and Bill laugh about that and the friendly rivalry between the two elite schools.

It was great fun to have Tilly be our guide to get us to her Aunt Jane's house. We chatted away and heard about her studies and college life. Again, just part of the family.

We turned off the main interstate highway and into the maze of country roads of central Massachusetts. We drove through small towns with historical names advertising local museums that recounted events in the American Revolution. The country roads twisted and turned over gentle rolling hills covered with woods, that beautiful mix of tall pines and mostly deciduous trees. Each small village or town had a town square with several steepled churches facing the center. It all seemed to fit my romantic, iconic version of New England.

Jane's home sits on the top of a knoll with a long drive. We headed up the road with Dee's house to the left. Barking dogs seemed to say, "Welcome!" as they came racing alongside the car, making us inch the rest of our way to Jane's. Jane came out the door and wrapped Chuck in her arms. I was hugged and welcomed too!

The next moments and hours were a blur. Jane got us settled into a cozy guest room. She gave us a tour of her small, beautifully designed house that had windows everywhere. From each window you could see the pastures or the woods. The kitchen and living space were open and centered around a wood-burning stove. It was serene and warm and inviting. The kind of place you can take off your shoes, curl up on the sofa, and stay awhile.

Within the next twenty-four hours Jim arrived, and once again the hugs of welcome. Then Maile pulled in, driving her old camper. It was so wonderful to get those hugs from Maile, who had made that *very first* phone call to Chuck. She also brought her ten-year-old grandson and his friend. They had all traveled from Minnesota! Maile had promised her grandson that on this trip they would go to each of the Great Lakes and at least put their feet in or maybe swim. Sounds like a fun-loving, adventurous grandma!

Marcia, the baby sister of the Taylor clan, also came that day with her son Jake. Again, more hugs.

Sometime that day, Jim's son Khalil arrived. He and his sister Tilly had a special bond, and Khalil was like a magnet for the younger boy cousins.

It was also fun to see how Jane made accommodations for everyone. The young boys and cousins used the tent that was set up on the lawn. Marcia had a cozy cot in the office/TV room, and Maile had the sleeper couch on the screened-in porch. Jim stayed down the hill at Dee and Ken's. Tilly had tucked her sleeping bag in somewhere, but I can't remember where.

For both Chuck and me, seeing the faces of all of Chuck's family was awesome! (The teenage word of the week.) There was a relaxed feeling that made us comfortable. I think Chuck and I could both feel our tensions and anxieties melting away. We didn't sense that we were creating any problems. Everyone just took our arrival as a natural thing. However, they were probably just as intrigued with us as we were with them.

The actual reunion dinner and party were planned for the next day.

After morning dawned, we started off at Dee and Ken's house down the hill for breakfast: stacks of wonderful waffles dripping with butter and, of course, New England maple syrup! Dee is stepsister to Chuck and half sister to Jim and Maile.

Later in the morning, several of us took a long walk to a pond through the surrounding wooded park. The teenagers were like jackrabbits, running ahead and climbing rocks. Marcia and I were happy just to amble along and talk about our kids. Chuck and Jim were busy taking pictures and chatting away. It was a peaceful experience to be walking with family—I felt as if I had known them for years.

By early afternoon, the serious party prep began at Jane's house up the hill. Chores were divided up into cooking, setting up tables, and bringing out chairs. All of these activities were greased with jokes and lots of laughter. Marcia brought out her guitar and ukulele, and began playing the guitar. Khalil seemed to have natural musical ability; he had never played a ukulele but just picked it up and followed along with Marcia. Old folk songs and fun jingles drifted around us as we prepared for the late-afternoon dinner. Chuck was also a helper bee, but he was busy behind the lens of his camera catching special moments and expressions.

More family arrived. Harriet, known simply as Hat, came with her husband, Tim (with his charming British accent), and Marguerite. There were more introductions and hugs of welcome. Hat is another stepsister for Chuck, and a half sister to Jim and Maile. Marguerite was the first wife to Charlie, and mother to Jim, Maile, Hat, Dee, and Buzz.

Then Dee arrived, walking up the hill from her house with her husband, Ken, and their son Daniel.

It was a surprise to have Marguerite attend, but we were so glad to meet her. It was another part of Charlie's history. When she got out of the car, Hat and Dee navigated her into a chair on the lawn and made sure she was comfortable. I noticed that she was a smallish woman with tight permed curls framing her face. I think I was looking for similarities to Chuck's mother to see if Charlie chose a particular type of woman, but no similarities jumped out at me. Marguerite was introduced to Chuck and me. Friendly hellos but no mention of the family connection.

While everyone helped themselves to snacks and drinks and sat around visiting, Marguerite called over to Chuck. She asked him to come sit next to her. He moved a chair over and sat by her side. In a low voice, she proceeded to tell him about an incident that involved his father in World War II. She said she knew the real story about Charlie going down in Tokyo Bay.

I'm guessing that everyone saw this talk between Chuck and Marguerite and wondered what she was saying, but no one said anything. I could hardly wait to hear what she wanted to tell him.

Dinner was a casual, delicious affair—meats cooked on the barbecue, salads, breads, and wonderful desserts. Everyone just helped themselves and found a comfortable chair. It had the same feeling as the family reunion Chuck and the girls and I went to in Texas with my parents. Many different generations, lots of stories, lots of laughter and acceptance. I hear stories of some reunions where families argue and old resentments flare up. At least in this scenario, that wasn't the case. The words that come to mind for me are *mellow* and *relaxed.*

We all helped clean up at Jane's, and then the party continued down at Dee and Ken's with a big bonfire. Everyone gathered around the warmth of the fire. At one point, Marcia with her guitar and Khalil with the ukulele led us in songs as the evening started to wind down.

Jim and Dee had quietly slipped away from the group. Then, much to our surprise, they reappeared with a *birthday* cake! Homemade by Dee. Loaded with flaming candles! Chuck was quickly taking pictures of the cake arriving. Then with a jolt, he realized that the cake was *for him!* The family had decided to surprise Chuck with a birthday celebration a few days before his actual date.

A chorus of "Happy Birthday" rang out with great gusto and laughter!

Chuck was speechless. He just sat there, so still, with a slight smile on his face. The emotion of being with his family was a gift he could never have imagined. This birthday surprise was certainly the proverbial "icing on the cake."

As I remember the events of this day and the surprise birthday party, I'm moved to tears. The way in which the family opened their hearts to us is a story about *who these people are.*

216   The Ribbon Untied

Our visits and conversations were just beginning to show us the inner beauty and uniqueness of each one.

Charlie had been the father to five. Their love and acceptance of each other made the circle of family bigger and more diverse. I wonder what Charlie would have thought about this group of amazing people—all bonded together because of him?

I found myself saying a quiet prayer of gratitude to Mary Lou for keeping the letters. Would she ever have imagined such a reunion?

The evening drew to a close as Hat and Tim tucked Marguerite back into the car to take her home. Finally, Chuck was able to tell us about what Marguerite had shared. We all knew about Charlie crashing into Tokyo Bay, either from Charlie telling his kids or Chuck and me reading about it in Wikipedia under the *Razorback* submarine's history. Marguerite shared that Charlie had been told *not* to go down to shoot at the Japanese ships. And he had done it anyway! This was the big secret. Charlie probably shouldn't have flown down to shoot the Japanese fishing boat, and he told Marguerite not to tell anyone about the actual circumstances. Little did she know that the story was already out, published in Wikipedia!

We all started to clear up the party. Jim asked Chuck to go with him to take Khalil home. Khalil lived with his mother about an hour away, close to Amherst.

This turned out to be a very special time for two brothers born just two months apart. Jim had lived in this area and knew the surroundings well. After dropping off Khalil, Jim asked Chuck if he wanted to stop for a beer at one of Jim's favorite bars, the Dirty Truth. The bar boasts thirty-five taps, so Chuck was all in.

Chuck says that as he and Jim sat at the bar, the bartender started to chat and asked how they knew each other. I am guessing that with big grins they told the story of being brothers from two different mothers and being born two months apart! The bartender had probably heard lots of great tales, but this was a showstopper! The Dirty Truth seemed to be a place where both of them were able to share some of their life adventures—and maybe some truths that very few people knew.

The next day dawned with another beautiful spring day. Jim and Tilly made scrambled eggs, and the Taylor clan had some relaxed time together.

Chuck was wanting to take some pictures of the five siblings. He requested that they all take off their shoes and he'd take a picture of their *feet*. (I had shared this with Chuck from a friend who did this with her sisters.) Of course, this request was met with laughter and then jokes about whose feet looked the best. They all huddled in a circle with pant legs rolled up and their arms around each other. Chuck took this wonderful picture—five sets of feet! The next was a picture of the five of them standing in birth order on the bottom step of the deck. Chuck set up the camera and I had the honor of taking the shot.

As I write about this event, I can feel the smile on my face. They were truly like little kids laughing and joking with each other. Witnessing the joy of my husband with his siblings was inexpressibly beautiful.

L to R: Chuck Eklund, James (Jim)Taylor, Maile Taylor, Jane Taylor, and Marcia Taylor. Siblings are in age order, oldest to youngest. Taylor family reunion, West Brookfield, Massachusetts, 2013.

Taylor family feet photo. Chuck always claimed he had the prettiest feet. Taylor family reunion, 2013.

The Ribbon Untied

21

Treasures from the Attic

*I*t was the last full day of the reunion with all of the Taylor siblings.

Jane invited Chuck and me, Maile, and Marcia to come upstairs and look through family history stored in the attic. Jim was off in his artist mode and had gone out with his sketch pad and pencils. It would be hours before he would emerge from his creative zone.

Jane's house is designed with this large storage room off her upstairs bedroom that functions like an attic. Here is where the stacks of boxes with family treasures were kept.

When Jane was planning to move into this house, her mother, Carol, was also moving out of their duplex and into a retirement village. Jane told us that as they cleaned and organized for both moves, it was decided that Jane would take all of the boxes filled with Taylor family history. I could certainly relate and relished what we might find.

As with any mystery, the five W's—who, what, when, where, and why—become important. We had discovered so many details in the letters from Charlie to Mary Lou. However, there were still mysteries around the relationships of the three women who loved Charlie.

In the early days of our visit, we talked about whether either of Charlie's wives had known about Mary Lou. Maile shared that she had asked Marguerite about any knowledge of Mary Lou. This had led Jane and Marcia to ask their mother Carol the same question. Neither of the women had any recollection of someone named Mary Lou. However, Marguerite disclosed that in the months following Jim's birth, some letters addressed to Col. Taylor would arrive. She recalled that she would put them up on the mantel. Once Charlie had collected the letters, he would disappear for a few days. I wondered if those letters were from Mary Lou.

A few days after Carol was told about Mary Lou, her only comment was that she thought less of Charlie. Jane and Marcia didn't pursue this feeling; they just let it be. Unfortunately, Carol had died of a stroke or heart attack a few months before we came to meet the family.

The timeline of Charlie's love relationships was a key piece of the story. Chuck was born in June 1944 and Jim was born in August 1944. Charlie's letters to Mary Lou continued into October 1944. The last letter even mentions that he hopes to come see Mary Lou in December. It appears that Charlie was continuing to write to Mary Lou even after he was married to Marguerite and Jim was born.

All of these pieces gave us facts only, without the emotions. None of us would ever know why Mary Lou didn't tell Charlie she was having his baby. None of us would ever know if Charlie *did* come to South Bend to see Mary Lou in December 1944, as the plans in his letter indicated. None of us would ever know why

Charlie didn't write to Mary Lou and tell her about his getting married to Marguerite. All these questions remain a mystery.

With that as the historical backdrop, we opened box after box. Charlie's life was there for us to see. Charlie was an only child and his mother, Vina, had kept a scrapbook filled with newspaper clippings about him. The book was falling apart with age, which had yellowed the pages. We huddled around it to see Charlie as a high school athlete, playing football and basketball, and running track. Next were the newspaper articles that told of his joining the army and going off to basic training. Every time he was promoted, there would be a new entry in the local paper that listed his accomplishments. To me, this scrapbook seemed to tell of a mother's love for her only son and the story of a small-town boy— growing up in Kentucky and Ohio, going off to war, and making a name for himself.

There were also envelopes filled with pictures of the Taylor family. Fortunately, Vina, in her organized manner, had written names on the backs so we could see Charlie's father, John Edward, known as Eddie. In many poses he was with several brothers and sisters—a big Taylor clan.

Other boxes and books would tell of Charlie's important role in the military. Each one of us took a box and opened up the past.

Chuck was immediately fascinated by his father's flight log. This was a large eight-and-a-half-by-fourteen-inch notebook that was about two inches thick. Each page of the "Pilot Individual Flight Record" was meticulously typed, indicating date, type of plane, and hours of each flight. Across the bottom were totals of flight time and his father's signature, Chas E. Taylor.

Chuck has always loved planes and knows them by sound, wing formation, and type. He has some recollection that his mother told him his father had flown a P-39. Would this flight log confirm that? At one point, Chuck had considered becoming a pilot himself. Holding his father's flight book seemed to give him a strong connection to his father that only he could feel.

Marcia and I found several of their father's passports. As we leafed through the pages, we could see all the places he had been. Inside the oldest was a very formal business card stapled to the front page which read:

Colonel Charles Edward Taylor

Air Attaché

Embassy of the United States of America

Moscow

Each passport held Col. Taylor's picture over the many years. We could see him aging but still the same smile.

Marcia looked at the pictures of her father and called over to Chuck, "Pull back your hair."

He just looked at her. "What?"

"Pull back your hair," she said again.

Chuck slowly put his hand up over his forehead and pulled his hair back so Marcia could see his hairline. "Oh, I see it," she said. I think she was looking for facial characteristics that were similar to her dad's.

I could relate to this since I had been told that my curly hair was just like my dad's sisters' hair, and my blue eyes were from my mother's side. I think most of us want to see a connection with our parents, even if it is a physical trait we may not even like! Somehow it seems that this recognition of familial traits is a bond and a linkage with the past.

Jane found the box with all of Col. Taylor's medals. This was filled with ribbons, badges, and insignia that showed how he had been honored. When I was doing research to find the family, I had discovered that Col. Taylor's DD 214 listed all of the awards. Here was the proof. One of the most fascinating was the Swedish Royal Order of the Sword with its yellow ribbons surrounding the four-sided metal cross. There was a bar with all the ribbons aligned and small replicas of the medals that were to be worn on the everyday uniform. In another box were the big medals and longer ribbons that were to be worn on the dress uniform. Now, these may seem like just trinkets in a box. But they are testaments to Charlie's valor, duty, and service to our country.

Maile found the large folder that showed the full history of Col. Taylor's active service and his retirement papers. It seems that many of the papers in the dossier were designed to be submitted for consideration in promoting Charlie to General. Here were letters of reference from high-ranking officers. They told of Col. Taylor's leadership and significant contributions to the progress made by the air force. And to our amazement, there was a letter from the then vice president Richard Nixon.

Col. Taylor had been part of Nixon's famous Kitchen Debate when Nixon stood up to Nikita Khrushchev, Soviet First Secretary, at the American National Exhibition in Moscow on July 24, 1959. At this international event, a display model of an American suburban house had been built. An informal debate between Nixon and Khrushchev seemed to have started in the model kitchen of this house as the two leaders viewed all the new appliances on display and discussed the merits of capitalism versus communism. The term Kitchen Debate was coined and used by the press to report on this historical event. We all had to laugh at this since most of our knowledge of Nixon was around Watergate. Chuck being the student of history could tell us all about Nixon's "Kitchen Cabinet."

Also in the folder was a letter from J. Edgar Hoover. It appears that Col. Taylor was leaving his post as Assistant Chief of Staff, Intelligence, to attend the National War College. On FBI letterhead, J. Edgar Hoover writes: "I did want to congratulate you on your selection for this assignment which is certainly a recognition of your outstanding capabilities and devotion to duty."

Deeper in the file were documents with SECRET stamped across the top, and then in handwritten script: "Declassified after 12 years." Knowing that their father was part of world events was interesting to all of us. Knowing your father was in military intelligence creates an intrigue and mystery around all the things in which he was involved.

We also found a spiral-bound book called *Submarine Chronicles, USS Razorback SS-394, January 27, 1944 through September 20, 1945.* It gives a detailed description of how Charlie crashed and how he was rescued in May 1945. This added new context to Marguerite's description. Marguerite believed that Charlie had only gone after a Japanese *fishing* boat. But the Chronicles described Charlie firing on the armed Japanese tugboat that was tending to a Japanese submarine in Tokyo Bay.

> *The damage has made Taylor's P-51 almost impossible to control and he transmits a distress call.*
>
> *Taylor's message is picked up by the Razorback's air cover of one B-29 and five P-51 fighters. Word of Taylor's predicament is relayed to Razorback. The air cover then communicates instructions to Taylor in contacting this lifeguard. Before Taylor switches over to the lifeguard*

frequency he hears the consoling prayers of the familiar
voice of his friend Jack Thomas.
"I hope you can swim, you bastard."

The account goes on to tell of Charlie maintaining control for long enough to bail out of the wounded aircraft. The *Razorback* was able to locate him about two thousand yards portside. Within fifteen minutes, the sub crew assists one very damp but otherwise healthy Chuck Taylor aboard and escorts him to a much-needed shower. The sub crew retrieves the parachute and quickly gets the ship ready as an order comes—"Dive!" A Japanese torpedo had been spotted.

In another box was a hardbound book that seemed to be one of the most complete accounts of Charlie's life experiences as a pilot: *The Pineapple Air Force: Pearl Harbor to Tokyo*. We could quickly see that there were many entries that involved Charlie. This document gives a sense of what was happening on the war front in the Pacific.

The letters from Charlie to Mary Lou, and now our information from Jim and Maile, tell us what was happening when Charlie was on leave. The complexities of wartime and the emotional involvements were coming into focus as we looked at the history of the family. All of the siblings were getting to know their father in a new light.

The attic treasure experience was filled with lots of laughter and talk. After a few hours of uncovering some of the mysteries, Jane asked if Chuck would like to take some of the artifacts home. Chuck didn't hesitate even a second. "Absolutely!"

Chuck and Jane then went on to problem solve getting these precious items to our house. Our suitcases could not carry anything more. We could purchase boxes at the UPS store and pack up what would fit. Just think: our historical treasure began with one hidden shoebox—of pictures, documents, and letters tied in a red ribbon. Now our historical collection was expanding into Bankers Boxes filled with memories of a newfound father and family! What came out of Jane's attic added a whole new dimension to *all* of the puzzle pieces.

The reunion wound down the next day with lots of hugs. And tears of joy. There was talk of family members coming to California to see us and more reunions in the future.

Maile and the boys headed off to find the next Great Lake! Jim took Tilly back to Boston. Chuck and I mailed our precious box on our way back to Boston. We then had one last night in Boston where we met Jim and his special friend, Jean, for dinner.

The trip that had brought us to meet our new family could not have been more rewarding. We were feeling deeply accepted and loved. Just a few short days before, we had been filled with anxiety as we landed in Boston. But we flew home bursting with joy and feeling excitement for the future.

For me, I had found new sisters and a brother.

My own sister is five years older than I am. She and I were not very close. In fact, after my mother passed away in 2004, she chose to no longer be a part of my life. I have tried to find her, but she seems to have chosen to keep her distance. I can't explain why, because I really don't know why. Then, when my brother passed away in 2009, I felt very alone—and lonely for family. I know I have Chuck and our daughters and the men in their lives. But on some level, I have felt like the last one left in my birth family.

But meeting Chuck's sisters and brother has *given me family*, too. Here I thought that my research about Chuck's family was a gift entirely for *him*. But what I have discovered is a boundless gift for *me*.

L to R: John Edward (Ed, Eddie) Taylor, James (Jim) Taylor, Earnest Taylor, Effie Dayton, Bertha Harbin, Mattie Swicegood. The Taylor clan of three brothers and three sisters. Location and date unknown. This picture was one of the treasures we found in Jane's attic.

L to R: Soviet leader Nikita Khrushchev (in the lighter colored jacket) and Nikolai Bulganin were entertaining US officials. This time frame coincides with the Soviet Air Show that General Twining attended. Party in the garden of Spaso House, Russia, July 4, 1956. This picture was found in Col. Taylor's records in Jane's attic.

The Ribbon Untied

Charles Edward Taylor. Yearbook picture from Wilmington High School, Wilmington, Ohio. This picture was another treasure found in Jane's attic. 1938.

Col. Charles Edward Taylor. Found in Col. Taylor's records. c. 1970.

22

Building Family Ties

$\mathcal{T}$he first reunion drew to a close with lots of good-bye hugs to all of the newfound relatives. We promised to send them copies of the nineteen letters from Charlie to Mary Lou. We would be sharing our history of Charlie. The letters had been the beginning of this whole adventure.

As I think about the study of history, I've been touched by some new insights just this last year. Chuck and I continue to listen to political and pandemic news during these strange times of 2020–21. We have heard presentations from famous Pulitzer Prize-winning historians like Doris Kearns Goodwin and Jon Meacham. Historian Douglas Brinkley of Rice University (my mother's alma mater) and distinguished documentary filmmaker Ken Burns unfold history with such in-depth insights. They all speak of the importance of stories of everyday life and the deep understanding of ordinary people during troubled times. When we study history, we know the outcomes. But historians look back and add *the contexts around what brought these outcomes.* A story well told brings *understanding* to the events in history.

When I frame Chuck's family history in these terms, I realize that after the reunion, we knew the outcome. We had found the family. But over the years from 2013 to the present, we have been busy *adding context* to that history. Each visit with a family member, each reread of the letters, each look at the family pictures, each study of all the artifacts of Charlie's military profession—all these have added new insights into who Charlie was.

The return home to California had our hearts and brains filled with images and memories. Chuck had hundreds of pictures to download on his computer, ready to process. We were overflowing with stories and pictures to share with our daughters and friends.

About a week after we came home, the box stuffed with Taylor memorabilia arrived. You would think we would have torn it open immediately and started to sift again through the artifacts of Charles Edward Taylor's life. But for several days the box just sat on the dining room table. Then we moved it to Chuck's office, still unopened.

I think Chuck and I were still coming to the realization that we were actually part of a much bigger family story. Our emotions were laced with the amazing journey of finding all of the new family members. And after finding them all, we were completely embraced by them! What were the chances of that happening?!

Maybe for Chuck, opening the box about Charlie made his presence too close. Could it be that the loss and anger of *not having known his father* was just too raw? I knew that in his own time, he would open the box and begin to absorb tidbits of his father's life again.

When we left the reunion in June 2013, we had no definitive plans to see family again—just the promise that maybe more visits could happen. The connection to family seemed to be real, but time and distance can take the glow off the emotions. We would just have to be patient and wait to see what would happen among these newfound siblings.

My teaching resumed with additional responsibilities that kept me very busy with long hours at the university. While I was at work, Chuck slowly began to sift through the box of artifacts. The flight log was the most interesting to him. He could track his father's entire career by date, every flight made, the type of plane, and how many hours he was in the air. Chuck's knowledge of planes and their wartime history was represented right there, in black-and-white, with his father center stage! I can only imagine how reading these flight logs brought him closer to knowing his father.

Phone and FaceTime calls continued with family members, always with the open invitation to visit us in California. Jane was the first to take us up on our offer. And in early 2014, she was on her way.

I love to entertain, so I was in my element getting the guest room ready, organizing meals, and thinking of things to show her in our area. We wanted her visit to be special. Our first visit to meet the family had been to Jane's for the reunion. This was our turn to host!

On one of our planned adventures, we drove along the coast of Southern California to Santa Barbara, about an hour away. It was one of those days that had Santa Barbara showing its glory with the winter sunshine sparkling on the ocean's gentle waves. The three of us just ambled along the sidewalks. Jane and I poked into many shops and tried on hats in a vintage boutique. Chuck took lots of pictures of us laughing and being a bit silly. We had a surprise waiting for Jane at the north end of the main drag along State Street. At the end of our walk, there in front of us, was *Jane* Restaurant. Chuck and I had discovered this culinary delight a few years back, and we knew it would be the perfect place to take her for lunch. A superb meal, a glass of wine, easy banter, and a newfound sister.

Over the days of Jane's visit, we engaged each other in exploring the artifacts in the box. One evening I was having fun preparing dinner in the kitchen, and Chuck and Jane had the dining room table covered with all the contents of the box—from Jane's attic to our table! When Chuck and I had huddled in Jane's attic looking at these special things, we were not really able to absorb it all. But now, with time, we could look at each piece more carefully and ask questions.

Chuck and Jane were like kids, pulling out things and reading out loud. Jane was telling and showing Chuck about their grandparents, Vina and Eddie. There were also pictures of the Taylor clan. Grandpa Eddie had brothers and sisters who would have been great-aunts and great-uncles to Chuck and Jane. Over their chatter I could hear them laughing. I peeked around the corner to see them sitting side by side, looking very closely at one letter. It seems the letter was from Grandpa Eddie to Vina Phillips. He was pouring out his heart and asking her to consider loving him.

Sept. 22, 08
Fort Wright, Washington
Miss Vina Phillips
Dearest and only one to me.

I can't sleep to night and I am going to write to you and I am going to write Just as I feal and you and amagine how that is if you was ever in love.

He goes on to ask her forgiveness (but we do not know for what), and to give him another chance. Apparently, she did!

Over a relaxed dinner, Jane and Chuck kept revisiting the artifacts. As Chuck laughingly commented about the love letter from Eddie to Vina, "If she hadn't accepted him, Jane and I would not be sitting here!"

Looking back at this time I found myself wondering if maybe the letters from Charlie to Mary Lou were part of the Taylor DNA. We now have three generations of Taylor men writing letters to express their love—Eddie to Vina, Charlie to Mary Lou, and Chuck to me. What a treasure!

The next day, we took Jane closer to home to visit the Ronald Reagan Presidential Library. None of us were necessarily fans of Reagan, but Chuck and I had come to appreciate the library. As school administrators, we had seen the value of a historical library for our students and greater community. With Nancy Reagan's guidance, the library had become a place to welcome and support educators. As it turned out, there was a special exhibit called *SPY: The Secret World of Espionage.* Fortunately, we were able to get tickets for our visit.

Col. Taylor (Dad, as we now called him) had been very involved in espionage in Russia. Maybe this exhibit would tell us more about how Dad lived in his professional life.

The three of us wandered the rooms, chatting and showing each other items we found interesting. We rounded a corner, and there against the wall was a replica of the US Embassy in Moscow as it had been built in the early 1950s. Certain areas of the walls were cut out to show how the Russians had built spy instruments into every nook and cranny of the building.

Jane let out a sound of "Oh, my gosh . . . This is where we lived in Moscow!" Jane had lived there with her family from 1954 to 1956. So she moved there at age four. On the model, Jane showed us where she and Marcia had ice-skated on the big open drive-up entrance that was flooded in winter for skating. Then she told stories of how she and Marcia had hidden under tables and played together. As children living in a foreign country with spies all around, they were probably oblivious to the seriousness of the world political stage.

What a serendipitous adventure to have in a museum! It helped us to know Jane better—and perhaps Charlie, too.

Our next visits with family just added more context to the tapestry. Chuck and I went to Washington, D.C., in March 2014. From there we rode the train to North Carolina to visit brother Jim and his partner Jean. They were such gracious hosts! They entertained us with a dinner party in their home to match the glories of Southern living. This was followed by a play at the local college playhouse. We admired Jim's paintings and enjoyed his artist's studio that was still being designed. We took walks and drives together around the area.

Late one afternoon, as we shared a glass of wine, Jean sat down at her baby grand piano and played "Clair de lune" for us! Jim told us that when they were teenagers, Jean had played this piece while Jim sat next to her on the piano bench. Even then, with no musical background, he could see the way the music fit together. He said, "It's like a painting—all the parts come together." Listening and seeing this music, he said, had been an inspiration for him to follow his love of painting.

236

On Sunday morning, we went to church with them and heard Jean play in the handbell choir. Afterwards, we met Jean's mother, Grimmy. She was one amazing woman—spry and energetic, and ninety-four years young! It was a relaxed, easygoing visit with no agenda. Just getting to know each other.

For me, seeing people in their life spaces surrounded by things they enjoy certainly adds to the depth of friendship. In terms of the gifts of having a family, this visit just kept piling the icing on the cake!

We were eager to see Chuck's family members as much as we could. We didn't let too much grass grow under our feet.

In October of 2014 we headed east to central Massachusetts again. This time we went to Jane's house first, and Maile came from Minnesota to join us. The four of us piled into Jane's roomy Subaru heading for adventures in Maine. Stepsister Dee and husband Ken offered us a delightful place to stay in their new, beautifully built cabin in the woods. Every time I think of this cozy cottage, I find myself singing and wanting to do the motions to the old summer camp favorite, "Little Cabin in the Woods. Little man by the window stood . . ."

The cold rains didn't deter us as we explored. We ate some of the best cinnamon rolls (Chuck's assessment) in a small village café, climbed to the top of a lighthouse that overlooked the Atlantic Ocean, and walked in the fall woods with leaves turning shades of red and yellow.

On one of our daily jaunts, we went to one of the many authentic small towns of Maine, Damariscotta. I was in heaven. I love fall and pumpkins. This town had lined the streets with gigantic pumpkins (1000+ pounds), which had been carved and decorated as people, animals, carriages, even insects! There was creativity on every corner.

We slowly made our way around the small shops, and I filled my phone camera with picture after picture of the delightful pumpkins. We celebrated Maile's birthday over dinner, and I finally had my long-awaited Maine lobster dinner—which was so yummy!

Again, more memories to add to the family picture. Sometimes I become overwhelmed by the openness with which Chuck's family has accepted us. Walking the streets of a beautiful village in Maine, I was very far from my comfort zone of California, but I felt so much at home with my newfound sisters.

The next few years had Chuck and me taking a giant step in a direction we hadn't anticipated. We had been in our lovely California home for thirty-four years. There, we'd raised our two daughters, had very successful careers, made wonderful friends, and had many good times. By most standards, we were set for a fulfilling retirement. But there was an urging for a new adventure. I'm not sure what nudged us, but we both felt it. What else is out there to experience? Did finding Chuck's family make us think about the possibilities of taking more journeys?

What would it be like to live somewhere very different? This is a game Chuck and I often played when we traveled long distances in the car. We would drive through an area, and one of us would invariably say, "I wonder what it would be like to live here?" Then we'd chat about the pluses and minuses of the place but never dream of moving there. Maybe this game of wondering pushed us to think more seriously.

In 2015 I was still teaching part time at a California state university. I would become eligible for long-term health benefits if I

The Ribbon Untied

stayed for a few more semesters. Was this the only obstacle to seeking more adventures? Maybe. Chuck and I began to dream of ideas.

Early in our married life, we had vacationed in the Pacific Northwest. Then, when our girls were young, we brought them back to Seattle, Vancouver Island, the Olympic rainforests, and other amazing destinations with towering mountains. Then our Jen went to school at the University of Washington to get her doctorate degree. That brought us back to this beautiful part of the world.

Could we find a place close to Seattle? What was the draw to leave sunny, dry, brown California and move to the wet, often gray—but green—Pacific Northwest? And did we really want to move? These questions kept circling our brains.

We decided to begin to explore possibilities with the attitude that nothing ventured is nothing gained. Over the course of a year, we embarked on several adventures to the Pacific Northwest. The area seemed to draw us in. We came in all seasons and would plan our stay for several days. We experienced time and weather on islands, in small towns, in suburbs, and in Seattle's crowded Capitol Hill neighborhood. We would talk to people and ask lots of questions about what it was like to live there.

One trip had us staying at a delightful VRBO on Bainbridge Island. From there we traveled and explored neighborhoods east of Seattle as well as on the island. But on this particular day in early 2016, we were riding the ferry across Puget Sound from Seattle to Bainbridge. We were struck by the beauty of the panorama: the Cascades behind us, glacier-covered Mount Rainier to the southeast in all its glory, and the Olympic Mountains in front of us. Chuck and I looked at each other and said, "What about Bainbridge?"

As they say, the rest is history. In that moment we made a life-changing decision that felt so right!

By the summer of 2016, we had sold our house to the first buyer and put our belongings in storage because we had not yet found our forever home on Bainbridge Island. I still had another semester to teach, so I needed to stay in California through the fall. But for that summer, Chuck and I, along with the dog and the cat, rented an apartment on the Kitsap Peninsula while we looked for houses. Our realtor assured us, "You'll know the right one when you see it."

This certainly happened to us. We found our forever home and moved in in October. I returned to Southern California to finish my teaching while Chuck held power of attorney to finalize the purchase of our new home. Retiring in December 2016, I was coming home!

I almost feel guilty about being so happy with our move. We had wonderful lives in California with loving friends, but this felt like the place where my soul needed to live. We have never regretted taking this step. As I think about our move, I realize that we are happy and have each other's love and support.

Mary Lou had left South Bend, Indiana, with a young son and started a new life. It appears from what we know that she had no support system. My heart breaks as I think about how lonely she must have been. My parents had left Texas and moved to California in the middle of their professional careers. Their family and friends didn't understand the need to move. But it was the best thing for our family.

All of these moves—changes in scenery, climate, or surroundings—give us opportunities to *reset*. Chuck and I both had the models of our parents who took risks, lit out on difficult paths, and sought out new life experiences. The moves our parents made brought Chuck from Indiana and me from Texas. When you enter unknowns, new opportunities emerge. For instance, Chuck and I both happened to work at the same summer camp in the mountains of Southern California, and we have spent our lives together!

Our new home became a wonderful place to entertain family and friends. I barely had time to unpack before our first guests arrived: my best friend from high school and her husband. Starting in January 2017, our guest room became a welcoming place for visitors. We love showing people the wonders and history of the Pacific Northwest.

Since our move, we've made some unusual explorations into Taylor family lore. Every once in a while, Chuck and I would talk about our families and remember foods that they liked and disliked. My family were foodies. Many a great memory is centered around our dining table covered with tasty food! I knew my dad liked anything sweet. One of his favorites was lemon meringue pie. My mom was a wonderful cook. Her pies were as scrumptious as they were beautiful. The meringues would have just the perfect brown on top and could have adorned the cover of a food journal.

Mom loved corn bread in milk. Because of her kidney stones she wasn't able to have too much dairy, so this was a very special treat. I can still see her sitting at the kitchen table crumbling the crusty golden corn bread into a tall glass of cold milk. Mom also made wonderful pralines. Chuck and my brother always received their own personal supply for a holiday treat. They would joke about who got the most!

When it came to remembering Chuck's mother's favorites, the list was very small. We both remember that Mary Lou loved butter and would spread it lavishly on her hot bread and pancakes. I think this love of butter has certainly been handed down to Chuck.

After finding Chuck's dad, we would wonder about *his* favorites. Were there likes and dislikes that had been handed down in the family tree? In July 2017 we decided to call the siblings and find out what kind of cake Dad liked for his birthday, which was in mid-July. Much to our surprise, it wasn't a favorite *cake* at all, but a pecan pie! Oh, I was very happy. Maybe I was blood-related to Charlie. This is my favorite birthday treat, too.

So on Charlie's birthday that year, I baked a pecan pie. Chuck took a picture of it and sent it to his brother and sisters. We may never have met Charlie, but somehow this connection made us feel a bit closer to him. Finding out little things like this make Charlie more real to us.

The first family members to visit us in our new home were Jim and Jean. We laughed and played and enjoyed the bounties of the Pacific Northwest. We would sit sipping the last of the wine on summer evenings as the sun set late in the western sky.

Since Jim had only lived with his father as a very young child, he didn't have too many memories. He told us that his teenage years were difficult. He was growing up in a world of women. At one point he was sent to stay with his dad for about a year, and then later with some uncles. He ran away from home and stayed with the family of his best friend, Jack. This was Jean's twin brother. So Jim was taken in by Jack, Jean, and wonderful Grimmy. (I think his artist soul was beginning to bloom, and he was trying to discover who he was.) Jim honored us with a charcoal drawing of one of our garden flowers that he produced in about an hour. It hangs in the dining room, framed, and reminds us of their visit.

Stepsister Hat (Harriet) came for a quick lunch visit when she was attending a veterinarian conference in Seattle. Hat is not part of the Taylor clan by blood but is a half sister to Jim and Maile. They all had the same mother. From Hat's perspective, we were able to hear about living with Jim and Maile, but she didn't have too many recollections of Charlie. Our visit was too short, but so wonderful! Hat is such a gentle soul with a strong moral fiber. She is calm, and I always feel relaxed just being in her presence. She had gone to veterinary school in Eastern Washington and lived in Seattle early in her career. Since we are relative newcomers to the region, it was interesting to hear her respect and appreciation for the beauty that surrounds us.

A second family reunion was planned for October 2018. Once again at Jane's home in Massachusetts. We were off to see the family! This time Chuck and I went early to stay on Cape Cod and tour the area before heading to Jane's house. We wanted to revisit the cemetery where Charlie was buried. To our delight, Marcia wanted to join us. She and her special friend, Steve, met us on a drizzly, gray day. We walked to the grave site in quiet reverence. Each had our own thoughts. I was remembering our first visit to the cemetery when we only knew Col. Taylor's *name*! This was before we found the obituary that led us on the path to finding Chuck's siblings.

On this second visit, we knew that Carol, Charlie's second wife and mother to Jane and Marcia, had died. She had been laid to rest in the grave site next to Charlie. We brought roses, and Chuck gently laid them between the two graves. We stayed awhile and talked quietly. As we were leaving, a man who had been visiting another grave offered us one of his extra American flags. It was perfect. I couldn't help but think that Charlie would be so touched to see his "kids" there together—having found each other.

We would see Marcia and Steve again in a few days at our second family reunion.

We headed out to Jane's, back across the country roads and small towns. It was a beautiful time of year with the leaves showing off their colors and ripe apples hanging heavy in the orchards. Once again, we were tucked into our cozy guest room at Jane's house. The first evening, Hat and Tim entertained the whole family in their "real" log cabin. We laughed, told stories, and enjoyed each other. This reunion was a bit more low-key, but just being together was great.

Our next West Coast family visit was with Maile. She moved to Washington from Minnesota and worked as a doctor at a military base, Joint Base Lewis-McChord, which was just about ninety minutes away from our home. This gave us opportunities to be with her more often. We were even able to celebrate Thanksgiving dinner in our home with her, her daughter-in-law, and Maile's newest grandson. Our Jen and Jeff were able to come also. Rebecca and her husband Artie were on their way, but a huge snowstorm forced them to return home. We missed them terribly, but it was great to have some of the Taylor family together.

As we held hands and stood around the table to say grace, I reminded Maile that she was the first one to say, "Welcome to the family, Brother." Now it was our turn to say, "Welcome to our home, Sister."

The next visit was from the youngest of the Taylor family, Marcia. She came in late summer of 2019 for a week, and we had such a wonderful time! We didn't need to do anything special—just "hang out." She and I chatted for hours and hours. I was so lonely when she left. Once again, I felt that special bond of sisterhood.

Then Tilly called on a Sunday afternoon.

"Uncle Chuck, I'm in the area. Could I come by for a visit?"

She had come from Boston and just happened to be hiking in the Olympics with some of her MIT friends. I quickly put dinner together. What fun to laugh and visit with the twenty-something crowd! Chuck and I were so pleased that she wanted to see us. And what a wonderful surprise visit!

In January 2020 Jane came, and I was filled with the wonderful closeness of sisterhood again. Jane brought Chuck the two boxes of medals and ribbons that Dad had worn. We had seen these when she showed them to us in the attic.

Jane remembered seeing her father in his dress uniform with all the medals displayed across his chest. She also shared that her mother was a perfect military wife and would accompany Charlie dressed in her finest too! I'm sure they were a handsome pair. Chuck was touched that Jane would bring him these treasures. Because Chuck had been in the army, he knew when and how the medals were worn. For the two of us, these medals and ribbons were very special pieces of Charlie to have and hold. This simple gesture meant so much!

Each time we visited with family, Chuck and I came away knowing just a little more about his father. Early on, Jim had acknowledged that Chuck was "*So* Dad." Then when Marcia arrived in 2019, we met her at the airport and rode by light-rail to the ferry. Chuck was wheeling Marcia's suitcase down the sidewalk as Marcia and I strolled along behind. We could see Chuck many feet ahead of us. She quietly said to me, "Oh, Chuck looks *so much* like Dad." I knew that look—the gray hair, the shoulders just starting to bend as he ages. I had seen it in the pictures with the attic artifacts. But I think I had been afraid, then, to share my thoughts. However, hearing Marcia say it gave me permission to see it and say it too.

In January 2021, we lost Maile. She had been in poor health and had returned home to Minnesota to retire. Her heart was weak, and she slowly declined. Her four children and her brothers and sisters rallied around her—but from a distance—due to COVID-19. Since she died, we have all been connecting through the power of email and each grieving in his or her own way. Through the email thread, Chuck started sending pictures of Maile. In the few short years he knew her, Chuck had collected so many images that captured her spirit and love for life! The other family members were so touched by the pictures. Within a few days, others were filling their emails with pictures and stories of Maile, too. Chuck and I keep thinking of her deep laugh and the sparkle in her eyes. She had a curiosity about life and a dedication to helping others. She will be missed!

The adventures with Chuck's family are precious gifts. We know there has been deep pain for each of us, from moments in childhood or adult life where words or actions have hurt and scarred us. As we get to know Chuck's siblings, we have been able to listen to their stories and empathize with their pain. We have had the privilege of sharing in their healing. Likewise, we have been able to share our family wounds too. They listen and support us in our healing. No one is immune. Through it all, Chuck and I have been blessed with acceptance and love from these kin who didn't even know we existed until just a few years ago.

For me, these visits from newfound family have added to the complexity of the Taylor family history. Chuck now has feelings of family that he had not experienced earlier in his life. Certain realities are true and sad, and he will never feel the love of being wrapped in his father's arms. Or the safety of a father who would help him get up from a scraped knee or go through a difficult situation. Chuck would never hear his father's voice reading a bedtime story or talking of his adventures at work. He would never hear his father's laughter or praise for a job well done. These are experiences that will not ever be. But the joys and love of the family we have found have added a fullness to our lives that we never could have imagined.

We will miss Maile and her spirit of adventure. For now, we hope for more time together with any family members. More phone and FaceTime calls, and after the dreaded COVID-19 passes, *face-to-face visits* with long hugs and more stories about *Dad*.

L to R: Marcia Taylor (youngest daughter of Charles and Carol Taylor), Carol Taylor (wife), Col. Taylor, Jane Taylor (oldest daughter). Ice-skating on the front driveway of the Russian Embassy. Col. Taylor was serving as air attaché from 1954-56.

The Ribbon Untied

L to R: Chuck Eklund, Maile Taylor, and Jane Taylor. In Jane's bedroom opening the boxes of treasures about their father, Col. Taylor. Family reunion in Massachusetts, 2013.

L to R: Chuck Eklund and Jim Taylor. Brothers born two months apart. Picture was taken on visit to see Jim and Jean in Salisbury, North Carolina, 2014.

Chuck Eklund and his "little sister," Marcia. Visit to Dad's and Carol's graves at Massachusetts National Cemetery, 2018.

The Ribbon Untied

23

The Puzzle Pieces Come Together

*I*f anyone had told me last year that I would be writing about my journey to find my husband's family, I would have "laughed out loud." And here I find myself drawing this writing journey to a close. Through the circuitous path of finding Chuck's family, I have learned the value of perseverance. My curiosity keeps me exploring and seeking new information to add to what we already have.

I can now see pieces of the family puzzle coming together. The adventures with new family members are far from over, and each day brings new insights.

When I first started researching, way back in 2008, I was motivated to honor Mary Lou. I believe I first had this feeling in 1972, the day when Chuck and I were perched on the edge of the bed reading the letters from the shoebox. I have never felt as if her story has been told or understood. Could my research lead me to finally answer the question, "Who was Mary Lou?"

There was a place deep inside me that called. I see her lone-liness as a single mother who had the guts to take her young son to a new place and start all over. I never experienced that, but my respect for her grows. She had the courage and determination to make a better life for herself and her son. I see these traits in Chuck.

To assist me in searching for new information, I found a need to develop a timeline to visualize the events in the letters. I took each letter that Charlie had sent to Mary Lou, and working in chronological order, I first noted the letter's date. Then I jotted down the key information that appeared in that letter. This graphic organizer helped me focus.

What I discovered was that the timeline of significant dates noted with "little notches" on the horizontal axis was only the beginning. This is how history has been documented and taught for so long—with years and special events marked in chronological order. But next, my journey had me taking deep dives into the "little notches" to explore the *stories* of the people who were involved in each event.

My desire to be the keeper of the family history had me researching, reading documents, examining pictures, and talking with Chuck about his experiences. Throughout this quest, I have encountered a rich history, and the lives of the people we've found have touched Chuck and me deeply. These last chapters have told that story.

But what I haven't shared is my thinking about how the connections to family pass from generation to generation. These ideas stem from my own childhood family experiences prior to marrying Chuck and from having our own family.

I believe that we all want to know our past. We want to see ourselves in those who lived before us. We want to see what is carried through us into future generations. There seems to be a desire to want our physical and personal characteristics (the ones we like) to be carried into the next generation. And those characteristics that are not as attractive? We want those left behind.

With these thoughts I began to analyze my perceptions of Haines/Taylor family traits. Understand that I am not trained in any deep psychological understanding; these are just my ideas.

What did I learn from the letters about Mary Lou? Charlie made several references to her holding her emotions back. Was this being an introvert? Or was there a fear of showing emotions? Maybe she was very reserved and more on the quiet side. What I do observe is this reserved, introverted nature in Chuck and in our older daughter. They are thinkers and watch the world around them very closely before they move forward. Was this Mary Lou, too?

A sense of duty and loyalty seems to run through many generations on both the Haines and Taylor sides of the family. Letters, again, are the evidence. Grandpa Eddie serving in the army, Col. Taylor serving in the army air corps and then the air force, Mary Lou serving as an army nurse, and then Chuck serving in the army in Germany and Vietnam. Maybe this is typical of the generations who lived through these historic times. I feel there is a common bond of blood that runs through the veins of those who choose to serve. My family didn't have these common ties, but Chuck came from a long line of ancestors who served our country.

Charlie's letters shared so many traits and behaviors that I see in Chuck. Charlie loved photography. In one of his last letters, he wrote about his excitement to show Mary Lou all the pictures he had taken, which he'd organized by the places he had been. This is Chuck to a tee! He is an avid photographer. His love of cameras started at an early age when he worked in the junior high school cafeteria so he could save his lunch money to buy his first camera. His joy of photography continues. He loves almost every aspect of photography: the equipment, the setup of the picture, the processing, and the sharing of his work. He sees the world through the lenses of his camera. As I watch and sometimes carry the tripod, I find his artistic eye quite amazing. He has taught me to see light and shadows and space and images through so many of his pictures.

My visual world is richer because he has shared his gifts with me. Our home serves as a gallery for many of his photographs. Sometimes I wander from room to room and marvel at his talent. I find myself thinking that his dad would have so enjoyed seeing Chuck's work. I can imagine the two—father and son—having long conversations, over a stiff brandy, about how photography has changed from film to digital!

The letters also hint at Charlie's sense of humor. In one such letter in 1942 he writes:

> *Happy Day! The goony birds have returned to the island. It is really touching (under the circumstances) to see them billing and cooing. At the present I am engaged in a comprehensive study of the situation. My thesis is to be called the "Life and Loves of the Goony Bird" or "How to be happy with what you have."*

As I read this, I realize my Chuck could have written it. I had seen this sense of humor in his letters to me, written almost twenty-five years later:

> *I've got a challenge to keep me occupied for the reminder of my tour here. Its name is Foote, and it's the new officer in charge of our section. He is out to hang me high. He*

254

doesn't like people with a bad attitude, and he thinks mine is amongst the badest. As you might imagine I'm justifiably proud of my bad attitude and its effect on the Foote. He is about fifty years old, has crew cut hair, is short, wears specs, and smokes a pipe. He likes to point the stem of this pipe at people when he talks to them. At first I had trouble believing he was for real, but he is convinced. Anyway, I dusted off my pipe and started pointing the stem at people. I got a rich reward of dirty looks for my pipe, but it caught on as a office fad, and everyone is pointing their pipe stems. My next project is to paint "Foote prints" across his desk.

As I read these two passages from a father and his son, I am struck that both of them make the best of difficult situations! They look for humor in their world—and they find it!

Chuck's love of reading is another family trait that came from both branches of the family tree. The letters to Mary Lou give evidence that both Mary Lou and Charlie loved to read. On several occasions Charlie would talk about a favorite book and send Mary Lou his thoughts about what he was reading. Then he'd ask about what she was reading. One interesting trait I see in Chuck is his enjoyment of so many types of books. I had never known anyone who will have several books going at the same time. One might be a mystery, another history, another a how-to book on photography. Whether the love of a pastime is handed down through the generations, I do not know. But I certainly see this love of reading flowing through Chuck.

When I was diving into the boxes of artifacts from Jane's attic, I was fascinated by Charlie's personnel records. His military career was notable, historical, and interesting. In the armed services, everything seems to be documented in an orderly and efficient manner. Every time Charlie was given a medal, there would be a write-up of why it had been awarded. Every time he was promoted, there was a written document of his personal traits that showed he was ready for this next step. One such document was from General Twining, Chief of Staff, United States Air Force. Charlie (Col. Taylor) was serving as air attaché to Russia. Charlie arranged for General Twining to attend the Soviet Air Show in 1956, and Charlie accompanied him.

This quote is from the thank-you note General Twining wrote to Charlie:

Dear Chuck:

I have now completed the official reporting on our findings with regard to our visit to the Soviet Union. As you know, I reported to the President, Mr. Mahon's House Appropriations Committee, Mr. Vinson's House Armed Services Committee and to Senator Russell's Armed Services Committee. . . .

I know this was only made possible by the unselfish efforts, loyalty and good judgment exercised by the group including you and your staff during our visit. The American people are proud of you and your contributions on this visit to the Soviet Union. I can assure you, too, that this sentiment holds for me as well as the entire Air Force, for I have never been associated with a finer or more competent group.

As I read these documents, I realized I was again looking at my husband. Chuck might not have been rubbing elbows with Russian leaders or top American leadership, but the leadership qualities that I saw him manifest in his successful career in education are the leadership qualities that are acknowledged in his father. Again, I wonder, what is inherited by nature? Do some of these personal traits, like leadership, come from our DNA?

The physical traits are more obvious. The moment I saw the military headshot photograph in the shoebox with the letters, I knew it was Chuck's dad. The lips and the ears were familiar. The squared-off jaw seems to come from both sides of the family. But was I seeing what I wanted to see?

Once we had found Chuck's siblings, the similarities of these physical traits were reinforced. I recall Chuck's first FaceTime phone visit with Jim, who looked at Chuck's facial profile and said, "*So* Dad!" Then his sister Marcia commented about Chuck's walk, saying, "Oh, Chuck looks *so much* like Dad." Again, I might be looking for things that aren't there, but for now, I see these traits in our girls.

Some personal traits seem to be shared among all five siblings. They have a wonderful sense of adventure. There is an element of the "daredevil and a twinkle in the eye." Charlie took the dive over the Pacific when he possibly shouldn't have gotten involved. Do his children all have this adventurous side too? As I hear them tell of their lives, I think so! They do not seem to be afraid to move out into the world.

Another personal trait would be their openness to new possibilities. They are all curious about the world. When that big white envelope arrived with news of a new brother, all of them opened their hearts to us.

Dad would be so proud of all five of his children. Each has contributed to the world. And I can say, as General Twining said, ". . . I have never been associated with a finer or more competent group."

Watching my husband with his newfound family brings me such joy. Whenever I hear him talking to one of his sibs, I feel a smile creep across my face. He has embraced his new family with a strong sense of loyalty and love. The scenario could have been so different. We were the extremely fortunate ones, to find the family and then to be accepted by them. That ideal image of the "Norman Rockwell Family" that Chuck once had, when he first saw his father's obituary, is a thing of the past. But this Haines/Taylor/Blanton family can embrace hurt and anger in its love and care. We see a family celebrating differences and uniqueness and continuing to build strong bonds.

The family puzzle still has a few missing pieces. But I'm sure *every* family has missing pieces. Many of the secrets have been discovered. The red ribbon that Mary Lou tied around her letters in 1946 was probably stained by the tears of a woman who had lost the man she loved. But she protected and cherished those letters and left them for her son to find so many years later.

The journey to find Mary Lou has brought gifts Chuck and I couldn't have imagined. Countless memories have been made. At some point, another member of the Haines/Taylor/Blanton clan will become the keeper of the family history. But for now, we are so glad to have each other, with Maile in our hearts. Soon, our calendars will be full of visits. There will be more hugs, more smiles, and more laughter, and more stories about Dad.

And just think of it: a whole family was discovered by the untying of a ribbon.

Collage of photographs with letters, 2021.

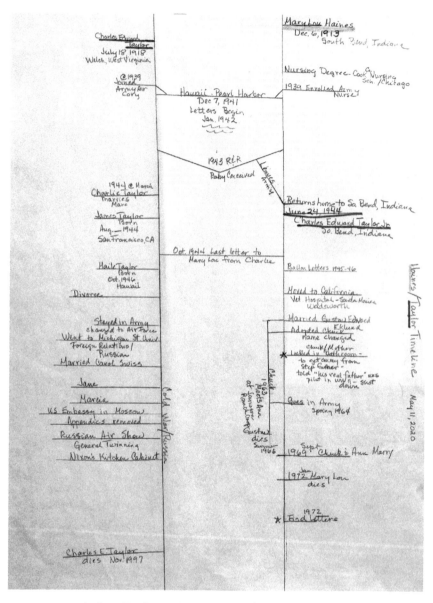

Ann's working documents to organize the family tree, 2008-2021.

The Ribbon Untied

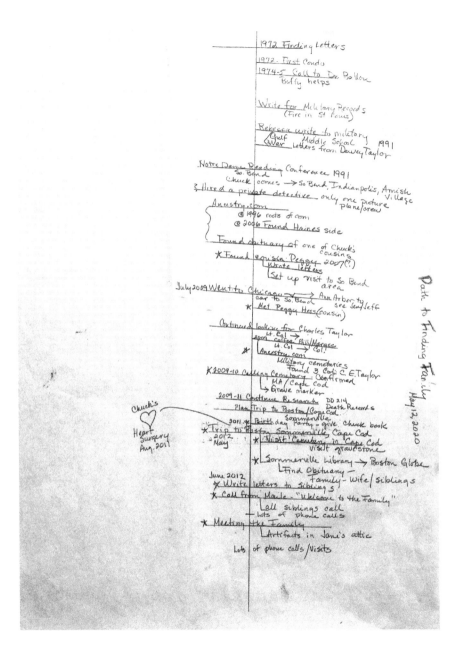

1972 Finding Letters

1972 First Condo

1974-5 Call to Dr. Ballou
            Buffy helps

Write for Military Records
            (Fire in St Louis)

Rebecca write to military
    ⟨ Gulf   Middle School   1991
    ⟨ War   Letters from Dewey Taylor

Notre Dame Reading Conference 1991
            So. Bend
    Chuck comes → So Bend, Indianapolis, Amish
    ¿ Hired a private detective   only one picture   Village
            Ancestry.com   plane/crew
                @ 1996 roots of com
                @ 2006 Found Haines side

    Found obituary of one of Chuck's
                                cousins
    ★ Found cousin Peggy 2007(?)
                    Wrote letters
                    Set up visit to So Bend
                                    area
July 2009 Went to Chicago → Ann Arbor to
            car to So. Bend   see Jen/Jeff
    ★ Met Peggy Hess (cousin)

    Continued looking for Charles Taylor
                Lt. Col →
    ★ 2009 cont. Lt. Col Bill/Margee
                        → Col.
    ★ Ancestry.com
                Military cemeteries
                    Found 3 Col C. E. Taylor
    ★ 2009-10 Calling cemetery - Confirmed
                L MA/Cape Cod
                    L Grave marker
    2009-11 Continue Research   DD 214
        Plan Trip to Boston/Cape Cod. Death Records
                        Sommerville
        2011 ★ Birthday Party - give Chuck book
    ★ Trip to Boston Sommerville, Cape Cod
        2012 ★ Visit Cemetery in Cape Cod
        - May   visit gravestone
        ★ Sommerville Library → Boston Globe
                    L Find Obituary -
        June 2012   family - Wife / siblings
        ★ Write letters to siblings
        ★ Call from Marie - "Welcome to the Family"
                    L all siblings call
            - Lots of phone calls
        ★ Meeting the Family
                    L Artifacts in Jane's attic
        Lots of phone calls / Visits

Chuck's
♡
Heart
Surgery
Aug. 2011

Path to Finding Family   May 17, 2020

Acknowledgments

This book started as an oral story. Chuck and I have spoken about untying the ribbon over and over to family and friends. Almost every time, our listeners would say, "Oh! That should be a movie—or at least, a book!" I never dreamed I could write this story. However, over many years of thinking about it, and with recent months of encouragement, support, and coaching, the memoir has become a reality.

My support team is so very large. There are not enough words of gratitude for all that others have given to me.

First, my dear husband, Chuck, who loves me and gave me the emotional space to be creative. His photography skills have supported my writing and made this a visual history. We have collaborated and relived the story often. We have laughed and shed some tears. Through it all, he has been my rock.

Our daughters, Jennifer and Rebecca, and their husbands, Jeff and Artie, have listened to stories of family history around the dining room table countless times. They, too, have found new family—aunts and uncles—and celebrated with us. They haven't met all their new cousins yet, but that will come.

My parents, Marion and Mary Cariker, were my foundation and taught me to love the family lore. Their positive attitudes and strong moral fiber modeled how to keep going even when barriers stand in the way.

Chuck's mother, Mary Louise Haines Eklund, was a mystery to me. It was my desire to truly understand her that inspired me to dig deeper. Through my research and writing, I think I've gained a deeper sense of who she was. My admiration of her has grown as I have become a witness to her strength and love for her son. Thank you, Mary Lou, for keeping those precious letters!

Charlie—without my even knowing him—has been the real driver of this story. His love for Mary Lou was written in black-and-white for all of us to see. Thank you, Dad, in all your iterations: Col. Taylor, Charles, Chas, Charlie, Chuck!

Finding Cousin Peggy brought family out of the realm of abstraction into reality. She opened our hearts to the Haines side of the family and shared the Aunt Mary Lou she had known.

Chuck's siblings and their partners have been like shining stars: Jim and Jean, Maile, Jane, Marcia, Hat and Tim, Dee and Ken. Each, in his or her own way, welcomed us into the family and made us feel loved and cherished. Maile's "Welcome to the family, Brother" rings in my heart.

This family also brought nieces and nephews, starting with Tilly, who was our very first in-person connection with a Taylor relative!

Once we found the Taylor family, we appreciated Grandmother Vina Phillips Taylor for compiling the scrapbook about her only son, Charlie Taylor. She was truly a keeper of the family history.

These were the family players in the story. But the writing journey could only have been possible with my editor, coach, and now friend, Jenn Hager. Jenn took me, a reluctant writer, from where I was and built my confidence. She found kernels of "good writing" and encouraged me. There were times I wanted to give up, but somehow, after I articulated how I was feeling, Jenn had just the right words to put me on a positive trajectory. Her energy and passion drew me in. She helped gather amazing professionals, Nancy Silk, proofreader, and Andrea Ptak, designer. They embraced the story and helped bring the pages to life. This has truly been a collaborative venture. And through it, my appreciation of the publishing process has grown!

Others I wish to acknowledge include the friends who have inspired and uplifted me and Chuck.

Barb Mixsell and Rod and Catherine Jameson were caring adults in our lives who loved and accepted us just as we were.

My best friend, Susie, whom I met in second grade, was that special girlfriend. We did everything together until I moved to California.

On my first day of high school in California, Chris, the girl sitting in front of me in history class, heard my southern accent, turned around, and invited me to have lunch with her. We became BFFs and shared our dreams and funny stories.

Chuck and I have built strong friendships throughout our lives. Each of the following people have listened to the story of the letters and encouraged us to find our family's roots.

Special friends Margee and Bill, who are always in my corner and Chuck's, have been close to us for years. This research and writing adventure has been more exciting because we could share the road with them.

Gayle and Rich are another couple who gave us helpful feedback on Chuck's letter to his siblings. A very special bond of friendship exists between us as we enjoy sunsets on their deck and laugh over wine.

Buffy was a significant contributor to helping us unwind the James Ballou mystery.

Cathy and Doug are dear friends who taught us the grace, "Thank you, Baby Jesus," as we picnicked with them on the lawn of the Eiffel Tower in Paris. Cathy repeated it in French, and Doug did the translation.

My amazingly talented teacher friends from White Oak Elementary School were always great listeners to, and encouragers of, my saga of finding the family.

Florrie Munat keeps our "Florrie & Friends Book Club" organized. This group of wonderful readers have also listened to my story and have been rooting for me to write it! Florrie is a published author, and I think she could see my reluctance to begin the writing. Through her gentle and kind words, she introduced me to my editor, Jenn Hager.

My girlfriends, called the "The Oaties," have been very unique friends. For over ten years, these eight women met every Friday morning at 6:30 a.m. at the same restaurant for breakfast—usually oatmeal. We laughed and cried together. We supported and loved each other as we navigated our professional careers. Though we lost dear Susan to cancer a few years ago, Margee, Ruth, Suzanne, Marlene, Cherie, Kerry, and I are still connected. Even though we don't see each other very often, our friendship is lasting.

Marla Jameson Reyes started the Memories of Moms Luncheon in 2005 after many of us had lost our mothers. Each year before Mother's Day, we would meet and tell stories of our mothers over lunch. The Mary Lou story was always intriguing to them, and they encouraged me to keep going with my adventure. The themes of perseverance and hard work of our mothers' generation were evident as we celebrated these women who went before us. Thank you, Marla, for this gift of remembering!

There are so many other friends who have impacted our lives and expressed interest in our story. The early days of our marriage were filled with fun and laughter with Frank and Jackie, Jim and Carol, and Ross and Debby. Professional lives brought friendships with Max and Jean. And now in retirement life, we appreciate Phyllis and David, Paula and Paul, Jane and Adrian, and Anita and Phil. They all have heard the story of the letters and cheered us on in our quest to find our family.

Finally, some special appreciations.

This work would not have been possible without the talents of the workforce of Ancestry.com.

Thank you to Dr. Gwyneth Milbrath for sharing her research about the nurses at Pearl Harbor.

I acknowledge the US Military for their comprehensive record keeping, their willingness to respond to records requests, and their efficient and timely delivery of materials. Special gratitude to the retired soldiers at the Massachusetts National Cemetery who shared so willingly.

Many who have crossed my path have heard me tell some part of this story. Thank you for listening and for showing your interest!

About the Author

Ann Eklund was born and raised in southeast Texas. At age fifteen, she and her parents moved to California where a whole new world opened up for her. Her professional life as an educator spanned forty-seven years. Starting her career in 1968 as a kindergarten teacher, Ann moved on to serve as a school and district-level administrator for thirty-nine years. She flunked retirement and returned to teaching as a university instructor for eight more years, until 2016.

Ann has had a passion for working within educational communities to analyze their current systems and examine new possibilities. One of her favorite sayings is "There are lots of right answers." Ann's fascination with the mysteries and secrets of family history—yet another system—has been the driving force behind this memoir.

About the Photographer

Chuck Eklund was born in Indiana and raised in Southern California. He served for three years in the US Army in Germany and Vietnam, and came home to marry his longtime love, Ann Cariker. Chuck continued his education and earned a degree in geography. For the next thirty-four years, Chuck taught at both elementary and middle school levels, became a counselor to middle school students, and later served as principal of a large suburban high school in Ventura County, California. He completed his professional career as director of secondary schools.

As a young teenager, Chuck became interested in photography and saved his lunch money to buy his first camera. This passion has led him to create many beautiful photographs. Chuck photographed the still life for the front cover of *The Ribbon Untied*, as well as many of the photos inside. He curated and prepared for publication all the photos displayed in the book.

Chuck is grateful to Ann for sharing the story of their quest to find his family, a journey that has given insights into his roots and brought many unexpected gifts.

Ann and Chuck have been married for over fifty years and have two married daughters. Ann, Chuck, and their dog, Gabby, live on Bainbridge Island in Washington State, where Chuck is active in the Bainbridge Island Photo Club, serving as editor of the club's newsletter.

CPSIA information can be obtained
at www.ICGtesting.com
Printed in the USA
LVHW070029031121
702272LV00010B/110